TICKET TO TIMBUKTU

an adventure

by Joe Lindsay

Published by For the Right Reasons

Copyright © 2013

ISBN:978-1-905787-69-2

JOE LINDSAY

All rights reserved

This book, or parts thereof, may not be reproduced in any form without permission from the publisher.

Exceptions are made for brief excerpts in published reviews.

Acknowledgements

I would like to thank Richard Burkitt and all the staff of "For the Right Reasons" for all their help in bringing this book to fruition. They have great expertise and enthusiasm.
I would also like to thank my whole gang of proof readers who helped to sort out my little errors.

When I was a little boy, my mother used to say to me –

"Och you, away to Timbuktu!"

She didn't know where or what Timbuktu was and neither did I.

Many years later, as I was nearing my 60th birthday, my wife Kate asked me if there was something special I would like to do to celebrate the milestone.
On a whim, I said "I'd like to go to Timbuktu"
and thought no more about it.
\-

On my birthday, Kate handed me a box, wrapped in pretty paper, containing -
A "Rough Guide to West Africa",
A travel shirt, with lots of pockets,
A silk sleeping bag liner, which weighed nothing,
A little wind-up plastic monkey,
And a lovely card with money in it.
She said "Joe, you only get one life.
This is your ticket to Timbuktu.
I want you to do it.
Happy Birthday"

With love for Kate,

who sent me to Timbuktu,

and was with me every step of the way.

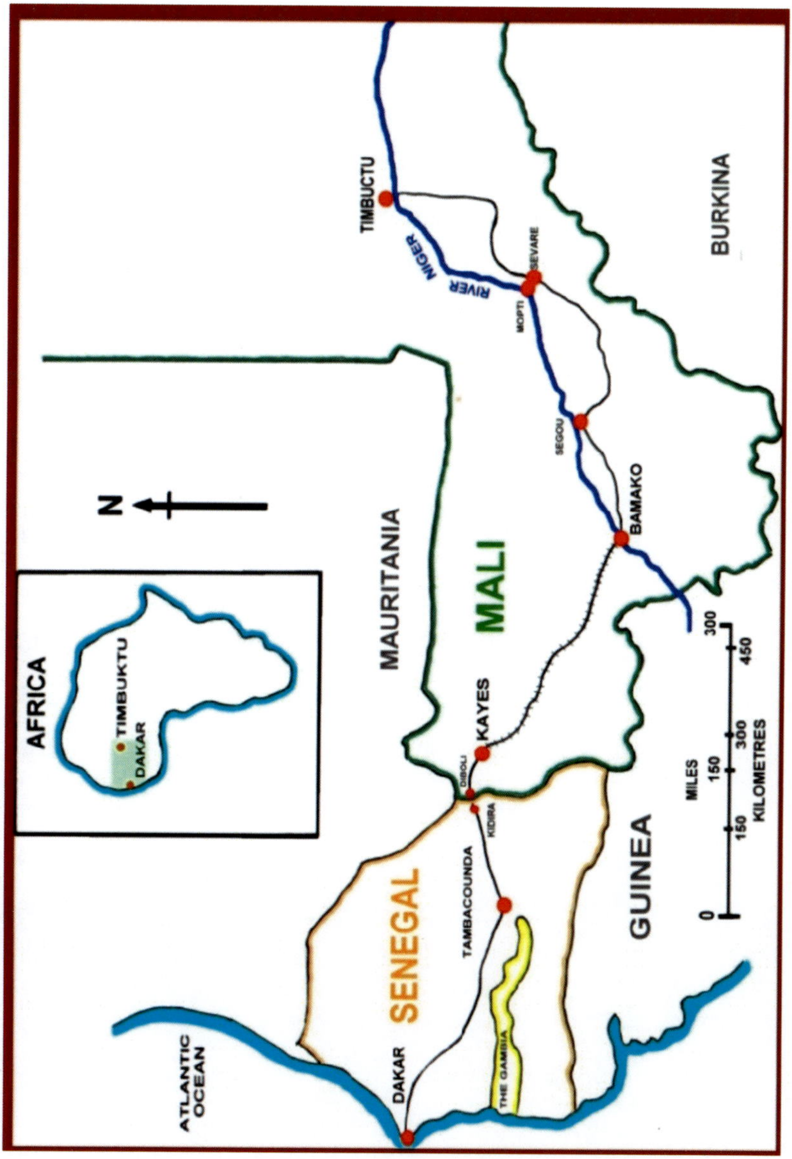
AFRICA
TIMBUKTU
DAKAR
N
MAURITANIA
MALI
TIMBUCTU
RIVER NIGER
SEVARE
MOPTI
SEGOU
BAMAKO
KAYES
DIBOLI
KIDIRA
TAMBACOUNDA
SENEGAL
DAKAR
THE GAMBIA
GUINEA
ATLANTIC OCEAN
BURKINA
MILES
0 150 300
150 300 450
KILOMETRES

Contents

1. GATHERING THE GEAR 7
2. DAKAR HAS NO SEAGULLS 13
3. BUSH BUS TO THE BORDER 36
4. TAKING A TRAIN 46
5. BAMAKO 69
6. BAMAKO TO MOPTI 79
7. PASSAGE TO TIMBUKTU 99
PHOTOS 114
8. TIMBUKTU 115
9. COMING DOWN THE MOUNTAIN 146
10. HOLD ON TIGHT 155
11. PANIC IN BAMAKO 162
12. UNWINDING IN AFRICA 168
13. A SETTING SUN 184
POSTSCRIPT 186

1. GATHERING THE GEAR

Although Kate had secretly done a huge amount of research and ground work, I soon discovered that you don't just go to Timbuktu, at least, not from the North of Scotland you don't.

Preparations must be made.

Almost immediately, I started to prevaricate, not really because I had misgivings about the trip, but because I just knew that there would be almost no time to prepare myself properly, ... and yes, I had misgivings about the trip.

The guidebook told me that the only real way to travel satisfactorily to Timbuktu was by boat down the River Niger. However, the river dries up in the winter and by mid-November would be too shallow for most boats. It was now October.

"I think I should leave it till next year. There's not enough time to get the injections and a visa and read up all the stuff I'll need to know," I announced, but wife and family were having none of it. They were as excited about the trip as I was doubtful.

"Come on Dad," said my daughters, "It's for your 60th, not your 61st. Just *do* it!"

Kate said, "Joe, I really want to give you this for your special birthday. I'm sure if we start now, we can get you there in time. Come on. Let's do it!"

"I'll do it," I said.

The injections were, it seemed, most urgent, so typhoid, hepatitis, yellow fever and meningitis vaccines were all pumped into me, and a stock of malaria pills acquired. Later, I would wish that there had been a vaccine for the common cold.

Next, I was going to need a visa. My idea was to fly to Bamako, the capital of Mali, and then travel by bus and boat, eastwards for about four days to reach Timbuktu.

"You'll be there and back in a fortnight," Kate assured me.

However, you can't simply walk into your local post office and ask for "A visa for Mali please." I soon discovered that I would have to work through an agency and not only would it cost a small arm and leg, it would take about four to five weeks for it to arrive from Brussels. That would be too long, and I would "miss the boat", literally. There were two alternatives. One was simply to fly to Bamako anyway, and take my chances of getting a visa on arrival. The guide book suggested that although possible, this would be a bit unlikely, and potentially embarrassing if I was turned away and was home again the next day. The other route would be to fly to Dakar in neighbouring Senegal, where I would be able to buy a visa for a few pounds at the Mali embassy, and then travel on east from there into Mali, and eventually to Timbuktu.

"But that's going to put an extra 700 miles on the trip and means crossing the border into Mali." I pleaded, "Maybe I should wait till next year."

"OH, just DO it!" was the chorus.

So it was decided. I would fly to Dakar. It would be a dawdle.

My *Ticket to Timbuktu* became a return air ticket to Dakar along with a booking for three nights in a "safe" hotel in the city, to start me off. After that, I was on my own, and with a stretched budget due to the extra time the trip would take, money would be tight. I was going to have to cut some corners. It would have to be the long overland route.

With mounting excitement, I began to assemble the paraphernalia that an intrepid traveller would need for four weeks in Africa. Three pairs of socks (one on, one to wash, and one clean), three pairs of pants (same system), three tee shirts (dark), one pair of lightweight travel trousers, pair of shorts/trunks, the new travel shirt from Kate, one large denim shirt as a jacket, pair of trainers and a pair of sandals.

That was the clothes sorted.

The rest of the essential gear consisted of the silk sleeping bag liner, (for health and safety), a mosquito net (same reason), an *alarm/torch* (very much same reason) and a little "magic" travel towel. The guide book was butchered to leave just the parts I needed, and added to a small English/French dictionary (West Africa is mostly French speaking). Since I decided that for speed and ease, I would only take a small day-bag type rucksack, there really only remained room for several packs of hankies, and lots of moist toilet tissues (both of which proved invaluable), some toiletries/medicines, and a notebook and pen.

I also took, of course, photos of my wife and family, to comfort me on the journey, along with a slim digital camera, a small miniature of whisky to celebrate if I ever reached Timbuktu, some little toys to give to kids, and of course, my new wind-up monkey pal for company.

The day before *The Off*, I tested out the gear, and with rucksack on back and camera safely hidden in a soft cotton pouch inside my pants next to my body-belt, I looked in the mirror and saw not the tall handsome rugged explorer that should have been there, but a small grey haired man with a round face and a smug look. I was prepared for Africa.

I thought.

Apart from some euros, Travellers Cheques, and 55,000 CFAs (the currency of Mali and Senegal, worth about 1,000 CFAs to £1) which a well-travelled nephew had spare, I was taking my credit card as my main source of cash, and decided that it would be sensible to reduce the limit on it from a ridiculous £6,000 to £2,000 in case of the inevitable mugging. So the day before I was to leave, I phoned HSBC, my bank.

"Hello, I'm going to Africa, and I'd like to lower my credit limit, to be on the safe side please."

"Certainly sir, I just have to ask a couple of security questions before we proceed. Can you tell me what transactions you've made with the card in the last two weeks?"

One of my many major shortcomings is an extremely poor short-term memory, and with mounting embarrassment I began to stutter "Eh, em, I'm sorry, I can't remember.

I don't think I ...."

"I'm sorry, sir, I have now locked your account. I can no longer discuss it with you."

"*What?* WAIT! I only want to reduce my limit, not take money out or anything."

"I'm sorry, sir, I cannot talk to you till you re-activate your account."

Now, in pure panic, "But I'm going to Africa *tomorrow*! What can I do? How do I re-activate my account?"

"Just go in to your local HSBC branch with identification, and they'll do it for you."

I had never, ever, used any branch of HSBC. "OK, ok. Where is my local branch? I'm in Inverness."

"Aberdeen, goodbye."

Looking at the telephone in my hand, I wondered if God was perhaps trying to tell me something. Aberdeen was over a hundred miles away.

As luck had it, I would be flying from Aberdeen to Paris then on to Dakar, so I would be staying with my daughter in Aberdeen that night. This latest setback meant an even earlier rise, and hopefully a quick visit to the bank before heading to the airport. All would be well if the traffic was light, the bank opened early enough, the queue was short, and the teller didn't ask any awkward questions. Otherwise.... there was no otherwise. I *needed* that credit card.

The next morning, Monday 8th November 2004, seemed like a dream. "I'm going to Africa. I'm going to Africa." ran through my head incessantly as I checked that I had all my gear, and dressed myself as a *Traveller* again. The family fussed around me with lots of advice, as if I was a *kid,* which I diligently listened to then discarded, and somehow they all managed to get me out and to the bank before it even opened. There were two other people waiting, but as I explained my predicament they no doubt could make out the slightly higher pitch of voice which accompanies mounting panic, and insisted that I should go first. Immediately the doors opened I was in and at the counter.

"I need to re-activate my card, quickly please. I'm catching a plane to Africa *this morning.* Please be quick. Here's my card."

"Please put in your pin number. Thank you. Your card is re-activated."

"*What?* Is that it?"

"Yes sir, anything else I can do for you?"

I was so taken aback that it had been so easy that I forgot to ask to reduce the credit limit, and just shoved the card back into my body-belt. This was no mean feat as it involved undoing the top of my trousers to access it (health and safety). If I was going to get mugged, they would have to take my trousers as well!

"Right, come on Joe, let's get you to the airport." urged Kate and off we all sped.

By the time I had checked in, I had calmed down to a tingling hum ringing throughout my entire body, but this was good. It wasn't panic. It was anticipation I told myself, and when my flight was called I was ready to go. *What was I doing?*

"Have a really good time, Joe," said Kate with a big hug and a kiss. "Hope we can keep in touch."

"Good luck Dad." shouted the family over the barrier as I passed the point of no return and disappeared from their sight.

"Well now," I thought, "I'm off to Timbuktu!"

2. DAKAR HAS NO SEAGULLS

Dakar has no seagulls, only vultures, and standing on the roof of the Independence Hotel, looking down seventeen storeys to the main square through the swirling tracks of those menacing birds, I wondered how, or if, I would make it safely back to my own hotel a few blocks away. It was getting dark and the vultures were gathering. It was my first night in Africa.

The flight had been very enjoyable, firstly in a little Air France "executive" jet to Paris, which made me feel pretty posh, even though the French cuisine lunch was only a cheese roll, then on to Dakar in a plane full of Africans, which made me feel very white. This was a little foretaste of the feeling of isolation which I would experience several times on my journey. As the plane taxied ready to take off, my stomach flipped. Another foretaste.

The heat had hit me as I stepped off the plane. There is an actual smell to heat like that, and as I was swept along with the crowd heading for immigration, I revelled in its novelty; hot concrete, and hotter people. You don't get that very often in Scotland. *Seck* was waiting for me, and he was a madman. He had no English, but did have a cardboard sign saying *Oceanic Hotel,* so I assumed he was there to transfer me, which was part of the deal that Kate had set up for my safety.

Seck didn't know the meaning of the word "safety". After shaking my hand, he led me, not to the taxi rank as I had expected, but through a series of deserted side streets, becoming less and less savoury, until we came to a gravel car park, with one sad looking Peugeot sitting in it. This was my *safe* transport. There was no speedometer, but I could gauge from the speed of my pulse, that we were doing about 80 miles per hour through the city. Meanwhile, Seck talked fluently, and constantly, in French to me, turning round and staring deeply into my eyes at every opportunity. I could only answer with a fixed grin, with my eyes skewed sideways, almost out of their sockets, trying to will nothing to block our path. I had no idea what he was saying anyway. Mercifully he slowed down a bit as we got to the hotel, and once the blood had returned to my knuckles, I became aware that I was understanding what he was asking me. I assured him that if I *did* need a taxi the next day, I would certainly contact him. My knees, which were still like jelly, suggested otherwise.

The Oceanic was an interesting three storey, old *French Colonial* style building, painted in deep reds, pink and blue. It was very pretty, but certainly not five star, and on first sight I had misgivings, but at least I was still alive, and had a place to stay. Later in my journey there were times I yearned for its luxury.

Having arrived in the late afternoon, and keen to explore my new world, I unpacked my rucksack and went out to wander through the narrow back streets to Independence Square, the main point of reference in my guide-book. The streets were hot, bright, and lively, lined with stalls and full of colourful hubbub, with smells of spices, fruit, chickens and goats. The square itself was huge, with shady tended gardens in the middle, and surrounded by business buildings and banks, where the *walking* vultures congregated close to the ATMs. The whole place was dominated by the Independence Hotel, a seventeen storey concrete pile which for some reason made me think of a tower made out of Liquorice Allsorts, and my guide book assured me that for the price of a bottle of beer I could visit the roof and if I wished, swim in the highest pool in West Africa.

This seemed like a good idea, but first I needed something to eat. At the bottom of the square, on a corner, I found "The Imperial", a super little mixture of café, bar and I suspected, due to the apparent oversupply of pretty young waitresses who congregated at the back, brothel. It had a little front courtyard with a few tables and chairs, separated from the public by a low wall, and this is where I had the first of many delicious omelettes and chips while watching the touts and wide boys working the tourists. The square in front of me was a perpetual melee of yellow cabs, vendors, tourists and touts. The noise was incessant and it was difficult to know what to watch next. It was fascinating to see the street vendors pounce on any taxi or car, which happened to stop for more than ten seconds, and thrust anything from carpets to chickens up to the windows. It was even more amazing to see that occasionally the window would open and a sale would be made.

"This is Africa," I thought rather smugly, "and I'm part of it."

Then it was time to take in the view from the Independence. The architecture of the hotel was quite exceptional, with all the front windows raked out over the square at an angle so that from inside it must have been possible to look almost straight down to the pavement below. I would have loved to have been able to see into one of those bedrooms, but such luxury was not for the likes of me. A beer and a look from the roof was what I could have.

Even that was challenging. The lift let me off at the *very* swanky restaurant on the floor below the roof, where I had to buy the beer. I was aware that I was dressed, not for dinner, but for travelling to Timbuktu and looked it, but the barman didn't blink an eye as he passed me a bottle of "Flag", the ubiquitous West African beer. Then it was through the little door and up the twisty stairs to the roof and the best view in Dakar.

The top of the hotel was not particularly prepossessing, being bare concrete with a few tables and chairs, and perhaps the *smallest* pool in West Africa, but with a huge 360 degree sweep I could see the whole city from the Atlantic coast with its many multi-coloured fishing boats, to the lovely little island of Goree, floating in the haze a couple of miles to the east. I could also see my own hotel, the Oceanic, like a Mardi-Gras wedding cake about half a mile away, and the winding backstreets leading to it.

As I looked, enthralled, with beer in hand through the criss-cross tracks of the vultures, I realised it was getting dark quickly. There is no twilight in Dakar, only day then within twenty minutes, night, and nights are *dark*. Although there are some streetlights in Independence Square and in the main roads leading to it, there are none in the side streets at all. They are pitch dark. With a start it dawned on me that it was no longer possible to make out my hotel, nor the route to it, and with a rising heart-beat, I fumbled in my pocket to reassure myself that I had my *safety alarm-torch* with me. This was really just a simple pocket torch, but with the press of a button, or removal of a pin, it would, I was assured, emit an "ear-deafening shriek which will immediately send any attacker running." Finishing my beer and heading down to street level, I walked quickly across the square avoiding any close encounters with anyone who looked as if they might be dangerous. There were many. I began to feel just a little concerned. When I reached the entrance to the first side street heading to my hotel, I stopped. It was pitch black.

The city has a population of about 2 million, and although it's cosmopolitan, there are still many homeless. The side streets and alleyways teem with them. Those leading back to the Oceanic were typical, and the people who lived there must have had the eyes of cats, but I didn't, and was about to switch on my trusty torch when I realised that doing so would simply advertise my presence, invite investigation, and culminate in the inevitable mugging, so with heart pounding, I crept slowly along in the middle of the street, hopefully in the right direction, all the time aware of the murmured voices of people around me whom I couldn't see. I *knew* that they could see *me*. Every sound or movement had my heart thumping.

Then suddenly I heard other noises, loud laughter, and garrulous talk in a strange language I didn't recognise, and it seemed to be heading straight towards me. I froze with the hair on my neck standing to attention. I couldn't step to the side since I couldn't *see* the side, and would inevitably fall over some invisible body, and I couldn't turn back as I would surely get lost, so I gripped my torch and was about to sound the alarm when *bang*, two Japanese tourists, all teeth and cameras barged straight into me. Once we had untangled ourselves, with great apologies, now in English, they wished me a good night and slapping me on the back, the two men disappeared into the dark as if it was day. They were completely unaware of all the dangers and terrors.

It was then that I realised that those dangers and terrors were perhaps not so much *around* me, but *in* me. Taking a deep breath, I strode out with somewhat quivery knees in the direction of my hotel, vowing not to let myself be such a wimp again. The torch went back into my pocket. I was however still mightily relieved when I saw in the distance the few faint lights shining out from the hotel, and it crossed my mind that I might not be up to this trip.

Waking up in a strange bed in a strange room in a foreign country can be disorientating. I lay stock still on my back, looking at the ceiling, listening to the sounds. What had woken me was the "call to prayer" coming from some nearby mosque. Not an unpleasant sound but not what I was used to. At home, our alarm gently woke us each day with a gradually increasing "Theme from Titanic - my heart will go on." which both Kate and I loved.

Here the call was a little more strident and overlaid with a fascinating, muted patchwork of street sounds, mostly voices of street traders setting up their stalls and the occasional bleating of goats. The light came through the slats of the shutters in bright flickering bars playing on the wall beside me, and I lay for a while, soaking up this new situation and studying the ceiling. The homes of many spiders had long ago been slung from light to wall, and across all corners of the room. The webs were BIG. I hoped that the owners, hidden from view in cracks and holes, were not.

I could smell toast!

Downstairs, searching out the dining room, I was amazed to see that there was a woman setting up an "Art Exhibition" in the foyer and adjoining rooms. I had thought that this was a rather downmarket kind of place. *An Art Exhibition*!

I began to take stock. Looking around with a more measured attitude, I could see that although the place was not the tidiest hotel in the world, it actually wasn't so bad, and certainly had charm. The colour scheme of soft yellows, and muted purple was nice too. It would do me fine. In fact I liked it.

I was still suffering a bit from fear of the *unknown*, especially the unknown language. Although I could speak a little bit of "school" French, I certainly had a lot of difficulty understanding any reply and this made me feel pretty insecure. Luckily, there weren't any other guests around in the little café/dining room and I was able to understand enough to get fed a pretty decent continental breakfast without attempting too much conversation with the young waitress, who, like the rest of the staff, appeared to be dressed in blue pyjamas.

Today, I was going to attempt to get to the Mali Embassy, to order my visa. It would be a long walk through the city, but I was relishing the prospect. In Dakar, it seemed, everyone walks. The streets are filled with people walking. If it was Scotland, you would think there must be a football match on somewhere, but here, it was simply life. Few have cars, and although yellow taxis are plentiful, they are relatively expensive, perhaps not to a Western purse but certainly to the locals. There are buses, but they are mini-buses, normally packed to the gunnels, and *very* uncomfortable. So most people walk.

If I'm in a new place, I like to walk around, getting my bearings and, if possible, finding the boundaries so that I know where I am, and although I could see from my map that Dakar was far too vast to walk completely, the area where my hotel sat was a promontory by the sea and was compact enough to explore in a day. But first, I had to get to the Mali Embassy. Outside, on the street, I had a look at some of the stalls. On the corner opposite the hotel, was a mass of cages filled with all kinds of small birds, some of them quite beautiful. I hated to see these little creatures imprisoned, and in other circumstances, I would have been tempted to buy the lot and give them their freedom, but I didn't have the money and anyway, the vultures would probably have had them in minutes, so when the stall holder hassled me to buy I shook my head and promised to return the next day and perhaps pay him for a photo.

After more hassle from a seller of some of the most beautiful wooden carvings I had seen, I decided to head to Independence Square for a coffee, and then on to the Embassy.

The Imperial café/bar was going to be a favourite place for the next couple of days. I could sit *safe* behind their little wall and take stock. Over a coffee, I studied my map and plotted my route. The Mali Embassy was about 6 kilometres north-west of the square, on the Atlantic coast and the obvious scenic route to it was round the coast via the Route de la Corniche Ouest, but the guide book said that it was a dangerous area and that muggings of tourists happened there. "Och", I thought, "What the hell. After last night, I'm not afraid of anything *during the day*. I'll go that way and see my boundaries.

I sat for a little while sipping my coffee, and watching tourists being approached by the multitude of street sellers, the most colourful of which were the girls with baskets of dolls on their heads. Each doll was made to look like a little clone of the girls themselves. They were very pretty and I promised myself that I would buy one (a doll, not the seller) to take home when I returned at the end of my trip, after Timbuktu.

Finishing the coffee, I rose, and as I did so, noticed that a tall young African, who had been sitting on a low wall near the café, got up at the same time. As I headed across the square I was aware that he was a few paces behind me. He hovered as I took some cash from an auto-teller, so once the cash was in my wallet I quickly dodged to the left and turned into a side street, but he was still there, no nearer, but there. It was difficult to miss him in his *David Beckham* football shirt which I had spotted from my café seat.

"Ah." I thought, "This is not good," and nipped into a baker's shop. My *friend* stood across the road and watched. By now I was getting a bit alarmed, and decided to use an escape tactic which I later adopted as standard practice. I dashed out of the shop and quickly waved down the first taxi that came into view.

Taxis in Dakar, are plentiful, yellow, and very varied, as are the drivers (apart from the colour). This taxi was no dirtier than most, but the journey to the Mali Embassy was long, dusty, fume-choked and slow. I could see why people walk. Still, I got there, not by the scenic coast way, but through the teeming streets. En route I was offered everything at the window, from chickens to girls. No room in my rucksack for either! At least I had dodged my first potential mugger. I could get the hang if this.

The Embassy building, when we eventually arrived, was very pretty on the outside. It was a white two-storey building with a *seasidy* look and could have been someone's grand holiday house. I was impressed, but before I could investigate further, I had to convince the taxi driver, in very poor French that I did not want a return trip to town, as I intended to walk. It was difficult enough for me to understand spoken French, and doubly so when it was in a strange West African accent, but I eventually got the drift of what he was saying. He was basically telling me that I would die! Terrible things would happen to me, and I would never get back to my hotel. I am, if nothing else, a glutton for punishment so pretended not to understand him at all, thrust the fare plus tip into his hand and said "Au revoir, monsieur. Merci" He shook his head and drove off.

Frankly, the area looked perfectly safe and quite deserted. There was even a little *Sculpture garden* close by, where some really good pieces were for sale. My priority though was to get a visa, so into the Embassy. Where the building had been pretty on the outside, it was quite depressing on the inside. Functional is the word. If you think of an old-fashioned Scottish Post Office, strip it of all but a table, two chairs and a filing cabinet, you get the picture of the main public room. Perhaps the Ambassador's office was a little bit posher, but I doubted it. There was one assistant in the room, who was very efficient and helped me fill out the forms (in French), took my money, and passport and told me to come back the next day. That was it. No arm, no leg, no agent, no five-week wait, no hassle. I was in and out within ten minutes and looking forward to my stroll back home via the University area, which would surely be safe.

As I was having a quick look round the sculpture garden, I became aware that a yellow cab was sliding slowly up outside the fence. My old chum the taxi driver had waited to get the fare back!

I did not want a taxi! I tried to explain this to him. I *wanted* to walk! I tried to explain *this* to him. I would be *safe*! I *told* him this.

He looked at me askance, and left. Ah, *now* I was on my own again.

The University area of Dakar is not like Oxford or Cambridge. There are no dreaming spires, nor boating lakes; in fact, you would hardly notice the buildings themselves, but the streets are alive with life and young vitality. The students, who throng the many stalls selling pencils, pens and all kinds of *gear* from tee shirts to calculators, are from all parts of the world and look like students anywhere, but without the scarves. I had expected a fairly down-market scene but this was vibrant and uplifting. One of the more surprising features was the many photocopy booths, where for a few CFAs a student could get his thesis reproduced. All this was *on the street*, and I could feel the energy as I wandered through.

All that changed as I left the university area and promptly got lost. The map in the guide book was reasonably detailed and accurate, but perhaps I had it upside down. Anyway, it wasn't long before I realised that I had no inkling of how to get back *home*. This wasn't so much of a worry as it was still only the middle of the day, and I could always get a taxi. I turned down a side street, thinking that this might lead to the shore where I could get my bearings, and there I discovered a little internet café which was great luck, because I had been thinking that I must make contact with Kate. Internet cafes are pretty much the same anywhere, and once I had slowly picked up the system of payment etc. I settled down to the task. Ah. The keyboard of a computer in Dakar is not the same as a keyboard in Scotland!

No QUERTY here. More WEIRDY and there were quite a few symbols I had never seen before! Having eventually fathomed the vagaries of the machine with the help of a young guy called Ivan, I managed to open my e-mail account, and there was a message for me! My heart jumped. It *worked*. I had contact with home. We had decided that the system would be that each of us would use the same e-mail address and simply e-mail ourselves. The other would see the message and reply, also to themselves. It may sound daft but it worked.

I quickly (well actually not so quickly, due to the weird keyboard) typed up the first of my many messages from Africa.

I am alive, happy, lost and enjoying the trip, but please don't send any more photos of me in the imitation fez!

I did a little history of my adventures so far, and gave the address of the internet cafe.

Thank you Kate. I love you.

Within minutes, there was a reply! I was actually in real-time contact with home. This was great. I had a *NASA CONTROL,* and didn't feel nearly so isolated now. We chatted back and forward for a bit, and I had to assure Kate that I wasn't drunk, but that the *keyboard* was, and she should expect the odd spelling mistake. Then with promises to keep each other updated, we sadly signed off.

Ivan was still there and I thanked him for his help. He was probably about 18 and was nice enough, a student, and friendly. He also seemed to be just hanging around. I explained to him that I was now a bit lost, and asked if he could maybe point me in the right direction. My mistake. He insisted, in good English, that he would show me back to the centre of town, which seemed very decent of him, but as we walked he began to relate his story to me. He was an orphan whose parents had both been killed in the civil war in Sierra Leone. He had had to travel on his own, grieving, for many days to get to the safety of Senegal where he had managed to get to the university, but was struggling badly to find the money for books, etc. It was a sad and harrowing story which took the length of three streets to tell, and although I noticed a discrepancy or two, I accepted it. Trying to hide the exact location of my wallet from him, I took out a 5,000 CFA note and gave it to him to help with his studies. He thanked me profusely, then pointing further up the street, said "Go that way," and promptly turned back the way we had come. Goodbye Ivan.

Luckily, the direction he had shown me led eventually to a place I could locate on my map and, since I was no longer lost, I decided to have a picnic-lunch on the street. With a banana, some crisps and a bottle of beer, I found a quiet, shady spot with a little wall to sit on, my back against an old building, and a good view of the happenings on the street. I drew a few odd looks from some passers-by, but decided that it was just curiosity on their part. As I tucked into my lunch with glee, I glanced at the sign on the wall behind me.

Hunger Project Senegal.

I quietly packed up and left.

My nephew, the one who had generously given me his spare CFAs, worked for the Foreign Office, and had not only given me cash, but had also given me advice. He said that when in Dakar, I should let the British Embassy know that I was in the country and tell them my plans. This, I assumed was for my safety, or at least would allow them to locate and identify my body if anything really ghastly happened. He was of an even more paranoid nature than I was!

The British Embassy was on the road to the point of the Cape, not too far from my hotel, so I decided that it would be a good time to visit, leave my card and talk to some fellow Brits. Making oneself understood, badly, in a foreign language, can be exciting but also wearying, and now and then you want to relax and chat in your own tongue, so just after 2 o'clock in the afternoon, I arrived at the gate, to find it closed. "Fair enough," I thought, "Security, and all that." I rang a bell and after a while, an African guard appeared and explained that it was lunch time, but if I would like to wait at reception, he would ask someone to come and see me. The reception area was pleasant and cool, with lots of leaflets about Britain that I could look at, but of course, all I wanted to do was talk to someone and tell them that I was going to Timbuktu. They would be impressed, and interested. I *knew* what Britain looked like.

No-one came, and after about ten minutes, thoroughly deflated and a little angry, I added my card to the papers on the reception desk, said a quiet and unfelt "Thank you," to nobody, and left.

Although close to downtown Dakar, the point of the Cape was quite different from the rest. It had a villagy feel, with shanty shacks, little *crofts,* goats, and goatherds. It also has a small hospital, the "Clinique du Cap". Where the environs of the university had been vibrant and cosmopolitan, the area around the clinic was anything but. The poorest of society seemed to congregate around the gates, and there was an air of despair. I did however wonder if I would have received a better reception here than at the Embassy.

Once you have passed round the southern point of the Cape, and are heading north again, you come upon the Savannah Hotel. There are many contrasts in Dakar, not least between rich and poor, and especially between rich Westerners, and poor Africans. The Savannah Hotel is not for poor Africans. Built on its own little spur, off the Cape, it is a modern, luxurious, Mediterranean style hotel, with pool, private beach and all facilities. Beer is expensive, possibly to deter outsiders, but it didn't deter me, so I sat in the lap of luxury, pool-side, and sipped a cool beer in the sun, ignoring the, mostly French, disapproving stares at my, by now rather grubby appearance. I would have liked a dip in their pool too, but not having my trunks with me, I decided that would be a step too far. However, I remembered the sign pointing down some steps to their private beach. It was wonderful to dip into the Atlantic, on a little sandy beach, which I had all to myself. It was heaven. I couldn't care if the security guard caught me. I couldn't care if some shark was heading my way. I was enjoying myself. After ten minutes, I did start to care that I might be caught, so out I got and dried myself with my tee-shirt, and now looking even less suitable to be in a posh French hotel, nipped out a side gate, and headed home.

In the Oceanic, I tidied myself up, put on tee-shirt number 3 and headed out to the Square to e-mail Kate, then tea at the Imperial. I must have been getting a bit blasé, since I dawdled over my fish and chips, which was delicious, even though it wasn't haddock, and had too many *Flag* beers.

When I was ready to head back to my hotel it was again pitch dark, but oh, I didn't care. I almost skipped home, occasionally wishing "Bonsoir" to the invisible people in the doorways.

Next morning, it wasn't the spiders that worried me. My head ached. Flag is an excellent beer in moderation.

This was going to be a big day. I would go back to the Mali embassy for my visa, and also look at the train station, and the Gare Routier, which is where the bush taxis leave from to go *up country,* so that I was ready for the journey the following day. I was becoming more and more excited at the prospect of heading east.

I decided to leave the visa till last, to give the Embassy folk time to do their thing.

At breakfast, where again I was the only client, the waitress asked me if there was anything I wanted washed. I was too embarrassed to admit that I was wearing a third of all I possessed, and that another third had been soaking in the bathroom sink overnight. I thanked her and said that I was ok.

The walk to the train station was pleasant in the morning sunshine, and I was becoming an *old hand* at Dakar. People near the hotel seemed to be starting to recognise me, and I attracted a few "Bon matins". A slight swagger crept into my step. The area around the station, to the north east of Independence Square, is very colourful, and the stalls are aimed more at tourists than locals. Walking in this area is more relaxed because you are one of many white faces, rather than the *odd man out,* but it is, of course, a happy hunting ground for touts and fraudsters. The entrance to the station is very grand, again in a French Colonial kind of way. It is quite impressive compared to the rather shabby low-rise concrete buildings around it, but the relaxed atmosphere changes dramatically as soon as you enter. Whereas outside it is tourists, browsing the stalls, inside is a melee. Immediately, I was joined by three or four young guys, all gabbling at me at the same time. I had no idea what they were saying, but they seemed to want to be my friend. Once I had managed to get them to slow down, and talk one at a time, I gathered that each of them would like to be my guide in the station, help me to buy my ticket, and carry my bags on to the train.

In Senegal, there is no National Health Service, and no unemployment benefit. There are many disabled, and not much work, and so these young men have to make some money any way they can. Helping tourists at bus and train stations, for a small tip, is one way, but since there are so many of them wanting to help, and competing with each other, it becomes a bit of a scrum. I never got used to it, and in fact found it more and more intimidating.

I didn't need help. I was only looking, and slowly explained this to them, but then they wanted to help me to look! Eventually, when it dawned on them that there really was no prospect of employment from me, they drifted away, and put the word round that I was worthless.

According to the guide book there was a train from Dakar to Bamako, in Mali, twice a week. *If it's running.* The journey takes thirty hours or more, and if you want any comfort it's expensive. A notice board said there *was* a train running that day. Unfortunately, I wasn't ready to go, especially since I didn't have my visa yet, and no cast iron guarantee that I would get it that day. It was Wednesday, and according to the old man in the ticket office, the next train would be Saturday, *if it's running*. I didn't really fancy hanging around for an extra two days, for a train that *might* be running, so decided to take the *easy* route, by bush taxi to the border, and then on to Kayes, in Mali, where I could catch a once-a-day Malian train to Bamako. This, I reckoned, would only take two or three days, and I might be in Bamako by Saturday. What could possibly go wrong?

So next I had to walk on, to check out the Gare Routier, which means "Road Station", and was about three kilometres north. I expected it to be like a simple bus station, but with an African flavour. I understand bus stations, and had no misgivings.

It was quite a walk, and I was a bit weary by the time I got there, so wasn't quite prepared for the reception. Several *helpers* accosted me even before I had reached the place, and I was soon surrounded by them. Now, this was *not* like a typical British bus station. It was more like a typical British car boot sale! There were no buildings, just a large space of waste ground, and rows and rows of cars and mini buses. Bush taxis, that is, taxis that do long distances in Africa, tend to be Peugeot 504s, mostly pretty beaten up, and not well valeted. There were hundreds of them, interspersed with mini buses of various shapes and sizes, all with groups of men, women, kids and animals in heated conversation. The sight completely overwhelmed me, and I needed help.

I *had* help, plenty of it, and with great difficulty, I managed to single out one guy, Daouda, among the throng of helpers and explained that I only wanted to see where the Tambacounda taxis left from, as I wasn't travelling that day, but would do so within the next couple of days. He led me, pushing through the crowds and along several rows, then pointing at an empty space, he told me this was the spot. He explained that Tambacounda was a long way away, and the taxi left early, though he couldn't say exactly when.

"How long is the journey?"

"About 5 to 7 hours" he assured me. Wow.

He also said that if I wanted I could get a mini bus. It would take a little longer, but would also be cheaper. Daouda was a good judge of character. However, looking around me at the mini buses being packed with what appeared to be dozens of people and assorted animals, with precarious loads of luggage perched on top, I decided that at 7 o'clock in the morning, facing a 7 hour journey in the heat, I would opt for a car, hopefully without chickens.

Now that I felt I knew the system, I thanked Daouda, gave him a small tip, and wove my way back to the entrance.

Since it seemed likely that it would be difficult to cash Travellers' Cheques *up country,* I decided to change most of those that I had, at the bank in Independence Square, but I was worried that there might be a limit on how much I could cash on any one day. I was also a bit concerned that I didn't actually have my passport on me, it being at the Mali Embassy. If I couldn't change the cheques, I would have to depend on what cash I had, which would be thin, considering that I was going into the unknown. I needn't have worried.

"No problem sir. Driving licence please. How much do you want?"

Almost as quick as HSBC, and I was rich again.

After that it was a dash past the vultures, and up to the top of The Independence for a beer and a last look at the view. It was great to sit and unwind a bit, out of the hubbub, but I still had to get my visa, and my passport.

Again, on the way to the Mali Embassy, the taxi driver insisted that he should wait for me and bring me back to safety. I must have looked particularly frail and weedy, since taxi drivers were always concerned that I would come to harm, and wanted to keep me safe in their cabs. Anyway, I managed to fend him off and got my visa and passport with no fuss.

That was me sorted. I had my visa. *I could go to Timbuktu!*

I decided to walk back via the university, and this time I *knew* I would get lost, but wasn't bothered. It was scorching hot, and I was melting, so I popped into a neighbourhood supermarket, "The Score". What a difference! It was like walking into a freezer. Bliss.

Since it would be an early start in the morning, I stocked up with crisps, coke, water and cakes for the journey, then just hung around for a while to get cold. It was lovely, but when I started to shiver, I moved on, out into the oven again. It was like a reverse of the Scandinavian *Sauna then snow* move, and probably didn't really do my health much good.

It was easy enough to pick up a cab at the traffic lights, but not so easy to get anywhere in it, and after half an hour of sitting in fume-filled limbo, being bombarded with offers of watches, carpets, chickens etc. I paid the driver 2,000 CFAs, and resorted to the pavement. I could now well understand why everyone walks. Luckily, the half mile we had travelled had got me to a place that I recognised, so all was well.

I headed for the Imperial for a bite to eat. Beer and sandwiches. What more could a man ask. In Scotland, in November, I suppose it would be mince and tatties!

In the middle of a mess of fuming traffic, milling crowds of tourists and hawkers, and general mayhem, many of the Dakar women looked so elegant. Not so much the *modern* ones, in their Western gear, but those dressed beautifully in dazzling multi-coloured swirling dresses, with matching turbans swathing their heads. They walked through it all, slowly, and gracefully, as if only they existed.

The island of Goree, just a few kilometres to the east of Dakar, had looked, from the top of the Independence hotel, like a place worth getting to, so I decided that a trip there would be a good way to round off the day. The guide book said that it was one of the main tourist attractions of the area, and certainly, by the queue waiting to board the ferry, I reckoned it was right. I joined them.

While I was waiting I watched a little white boy of about four, crawling on the floor. An old African woman yelled at him to get up, and he ran, blubbing to his young mum. Being a Grandpa, that tugged at my heartstrings, so I had a few words, and discovered that the *mum* was actually his nanny, and that he, and his older sister were from Bonhill near Glasgow! The old woman explained that the floor was dirty, and that the little boy was sure to lick his fingers and get ill. He was still crying, so, to placate him, I gave him and his sister a small *magic slate* each. I had brought half a dozen of them with me for this very purpose. A magic slate? It's a little sheet of cellophane backed with a special cardboard, such that when you write on it with a small pointed stick, it leaves a mark, which can be erased by separating the cardboard and cellophane. It can be used again and again. It's magic, and I don't know how it works. It certainly *worked its magic*, and there were smiles all round again. I also gave the nanny a couple of my wet-wipes for the little fingers. More smiles. It seemed that Goree was not only a tourist trap, but also home to a few ex-pats who commute to work in Dakar. His father was an engineer, and the family lived on the island.

The ferry is quite small, holding maybe about a hundred passengers max, and most of the seating is up top. The clientele appeared to be mainly African tourists. As we approached the little harbour on the island, about ten local boys jumped into the water in front of the ferry. The water was crystal clear, and those who had made the trip before knew what was expected of them. They threw coins from the boat, and the boys scrambled to get them..... in about fifteen feet of water. These kids were good swimmers! Because the water was so clear, we could watch them all the way down, and marvel at how long they could stay there. We were gasping more than they were. Of course, everyone had to throw at least one coin, and the lads made quite a haul. With several ferries per day, they make a fair wage, but occasionally, some must get run over.

Goree is about 300 metres from East to West, and 800 metres from North to South, so it's not big, but is packed with interest, and I fell in love with it, even before I had got off the ferry. Nestling beside the pier, is a beautiful little yellow, soft sand beach, surrounded by a few cafes, and low rise buildings with red roofs, and soft-yellow walls. The island is interspersed with trees, giving splashes of green which softens the view even more, and at both north and south ends, there is a small rise, the north housing an old fort/museum, and the south a *Castle,* with wartime gun emplacements. The scale is so small, that most of it can be seen from the boat.

Since the afternoon was wearing on, I decided to have a short walk around then have a meal before getting the 7 p.m. ferry back. This would be the second last ferry, and it would be dark by then. The island has a small indigenous population of a few hundred or so, which seemed to be mostly kids and cats, and the atmosphere was very laid back, although even here there were a few hustlers, but they weren't very good at their trade. I asked around about accommodation, and discovered that the wonderfully named "Hostellerie du Chevalier de Bouffliers" was the best, almost the only place to stay. It had a little restaurant overlooking the beach, and looked idyllic. I decided that if at all possible, I would have a night there on my return from Timbuktu. Although I hadn't yet seen much of the island, a meal at one of the beach cafes seemed a good idea, to allow me to soak up the atmosphere. I chose the wrong cafe.

As soon as I had ordered my *Chicken Yassa,* Mama Kine began to hustle me to buy one of the many necklaces that she was wearing round her neck. She owned the place and supplemented her income from the food, with a few pounds from trinkets. I tried to tell her that I didn't want one now, but would be back in a couple of weeks. This was no good. She wanted a sale *now*, so sat with me throughout the whole meal, alternately asking about my wife, my home, my beliefs, and then asking if I was ready to buy a necklace. Eventually, I had to excuse myself, pay the bill and head off round the corner for a bit of peace. I vowed that whether I came back to the island or not, I would never sit in that cafe again. The chicken Yassa was good though.

Eventually I needed a beer, and headed for a different cafe, overlooking a small open area near the beach, where some local lads were playing Boule, which appeared to be a French version of Bowls, but with the balls being thrown, rather than rolled. This would be a perfect end to the trip, sitting sipping cold beer in the balmy early evening air. Most of the tourists and visitors had left, so I had the cafe to myself. Feet up, I revelled in the peace, occasionally broken by a shout of victory from the boys. It was then that I realised that soon it would be dark, and I might need my torch for the journey home. I had it with me, at the bottom of my rucksack, so I delved in to retrieve it. Out came the torch, but left behind the ring, the string, and the pin, which when pulled, would set off the alarm. The alarm went off! Although it may not have been loud enough to "Scare off any attacker", it certainly scared me.

The boys, playing boule, stopped, and as if choreographed, all turned and looked at me, broke into wide grins, and started running about like headless chickens shouting "Police! Police!" Meanwhile, I was scrabbling in my bag to find the wayward ring, string, and pin, which had become snagged at the bottom. Eventually, with much embarrassment, I managed to silence the thing, and when I looked up, the lads were all lying on the ground laughing. Ok, I was calmer now, and I gave them a sheepish smile. One came over, gave me a *High Five,* and then they, still with an occasional giggle, carried on with their game. To them I was just another daft tourist, but now I felt a little part of the *scene,* and was feeling so mellow that I decided to wait for the last ferry at 7.30 p.m.

Since most of the touts, tourists, visitors and commuters had already headed home to Dakar, the ferry was almost deserted, and the dozen or so other passengers stayed down below. I had the top deck all to myself, and the opportunity to do something I had dreamed of for ages. Jammed right up in the pointy bit of the bow, I stretched out my arms, and *flew* over the black waters towards the twinkling lights of Dakar. Leonardo di Caprio had Kate Winslet with him when he did it. I had my Kate. The boat may not have been as big as the Titanic, and we may not have been heading for New York, but at least it was balmy warm, and there were no icebergs to break the spell.

I got a full five minutes of bliss, which I will remember always, before someone appeared and told me it was dangerous.

Back in Dakar I e-mailed Kate and told her about our *Titanic* moment. We had a small chat and then I warned her that as I would be on the road, it might be a few days before we had contact again. We kissed by internet, and said goodnight.

Back at the hotel, the old receptionist man told me that I should leave no later than 6.30 in the morning, if I wanted to catch the bush taxi to Tambacounda. There would be no time for breakfast. Thank goodness for the Chicken Yassa on Goree. That might keep me going till I could have a bite to eat. The crisps etc. that I had bought for lunch en route, would have to be breakfast instead.

To bed, but I didn't sleep much. The next day I would leave the *safety* of Dakar.

3. BUSH BUS TO THE BORDER

Up before dawn, then out into the dark street. I had become much more relaxed about walking in the dark, and there is a very special feeling being out in a strange place so early in the morning. People were starting to stir. Things were just beginning to happen. Sleepy-eyed people glanced at me in the half-light, and occasionally there was a smile. It was too early for hassle or hustle.

Even at that time in the morning, taxis were plentiful, and I was soon at the Gare Routier. Here the scene was not so calm. In fact it was chaos! At least it appeared that way to my inexperienced eye. Immediately several touts homed in, but since I had sussed out the system the day before, there was no need for them, I thought. I dodged them, or shrugged them off. I was 60 for God's sake. Surely I could catch a bus. Then it dawned on me that I wasn't sure that I was in the right line of cars for Tambacounda. In fact it might not even be the right *section* of this vast melee of cars and people. I was lost.

The touts, whose job it is to lead people to the correct spot do not congregate *inside* the Gare Routier. That would be daft. They, of course, congregate outside, to pick up customers as they arrive. There were no touts around me, and although there were plenty of other people, they either didn't understand me, or were too busy to help. I was starting to panic. Time was wearing on, and if the taxi left for Tamba without me, it would mean another day in Dakar. More and more frantically, I started to accost everyone and anyone, to no avail, until a little boy, who must have had a good English teacher took pity on me.

"Come with me." and I followed, gladly. He led me to his Grampa, who obviously had been a tout himself in his day, and knew everyone. He rather unceremoniously dragged me by the sleeve to a 504 beside a very small "Tamba" sign which I had missed, and I was pushed into the middle of the back seat between two young men, along with my rucksack. Bush taxis are normally the province of the local African population. Tourists are not considered to be *special*. They are a bother.

The Peugeot 504 is ideally suited to the task of bush taxi. It's tough, and can seat 7 passengers, 10 at a push. I was lucky. It was a quiet day with only seven in the car. In front of me were three people, and in front of them was the driver, and one privileged person with room to breathe. In the very middle was a young woman with a baby, and a cough.

At 7.15 a.m. we were off, and I mentally waved "Au revoir" to Dakar.

At first, I was amazed at how good the main roads in Senegal were. Good tarmac, and pretty smooth. Perhaps this was going to be quick and easy. Then it changed. About 8 km. outside Dakar, the maintenance regime obviously came to a halt, and the road became 75 per cent pothole, 25 per cent tarmac. The potholes appeared to be mostly on our side, but that didn't worry our driver. He simply drove on the other side. He would wait until the last moment, as a lorry approached us, and just as the scream was rising in my throat would jam on the brakes and veer out of the way, clattering and banging over the potholes. He did this a lot, and was obviously practised at it. My travelling companions hardly seemed to notice, and simply sat silently staring ahead. Perhaps they were praying.

After an hour of this, even I became a bit blasé, and noticed that I was getting really hungry, and dry. Since we still had at least another 5 hours' travel to do, with or without stops, I reckoned this would be a good time to sneak out some crisps and a drink.

First was my bottle of water, and to be friendly, I offered it to the lad on my right.

Adama said "Thank you, but it is Ramadan, and we don't drink or eat from sunrise to sunset."

"Nothing? None of you?"

"No, none of us will eat or drink till we are in Tamba tonight, but please, you carry on. We will not be offended."

Ah, I had had no breakfast, I was in a car full of Muslims during Ramadan, the journey would be another 5 hours at least, and I was hungry!

I couldn't do it. I couldn't bring myself to guzzle while they fasted, especially as I thought that perhaps the crisps I had bought were Smokey Bacon. And so, I too fasted. Occasionally I would surreptitiously sneak a sip of water from my bottle. Well as surreptitiously as I could, being squashed in the middle of the back seat of a car, where if one person breathed, the other two had to move over a bit. There were a couple of stops of course, but these were not for eating, but praying.

I prayed - for the journey to end.

At this time, I was introduced to the plastic kettle.

One would think that a plastic kettle would not be a common item, due to an obvious flaw in design, but they were ubiquitous. Almost always yellow and green striped, and of a good size, they were actually quite pretty, and of course were not for boiling water, not that I ever saw anyway, but were intended to facilitate the washing of head, hands, feet and other bits, prior to prayer. Whether my companions carried their own kettles with them, or they were already there, and filled when we stopped, I never actually noticed, but I did appreciate their practicality. One fill was adequate for at least two people, and washing could be done anywhere, if one wanted to be private. Watching all this at least took my mind off my hunger for a couple of minutes, and at about 4.00 p.m. we arrived in Tambacounda. The journey had been more than 8 hours! My hunger had passed by then and I was into the secondary stage of utter resignation and weariness, as I was dropped off in the centre of town.

Tambacounda has a population of about 80,000, and is the regional capital. There is a train station, post office, airport, public park, and very little tarmac. The first impression is of long vistas down the straight, grid system, red dust streets, with people walking, always walking.

In the state I was in, I registered little of this, and appreciated little of what I saw. I needed to eat! So, I hailed one of the many yellow cabs cruising around, and headed for the Hotel Niji, which was recommended by the guide-book. Fortunately, the hotel, a low-rise, rather rambling old concrete structure, turned out to be perfectly adequate, though basic, and I was soon holed up in my pick of the best rooms, drinking a beer, and stuffing crisps, biscuits, and cakes into my face. It was then that I started to talk to my little wind-up monkey. Set in motion, it would chatter across the table about a foot, then stop and appear to be looking at me, waiting for me to say something. Perhaps I was going crazy, but at least it was company.

Since I intended to leave early in the morning by another bush taxi (the thought put a shudder through me), I knew I would have no time to properly explore Tamba, but I had set my mind on having a swim at the Asta Kebe hotel. This purported to be the poshest hotel in Tamba, and had an outdoor pool, which seemed like a dream. The system, supposedly, was the same as the Independence – buy a drink, have a swim.

It wasn't far away, so off up the road with my little travel towel, and trunks, and a dream in my head of sun-beds, children's laughter, and cocktails from the bar. The dream stayed a dream. The Asta Kebe was indeed impressive, in a small way, for the area, with a modern main block and an enticing pool at the back, glimpsed through the security gates, but there was no-one there! At the reception desk, in the attractive entrance hall, I rang an old fashioned brass hotel bell. Nobody came. I was beginning to think that perhaps the place was run by the British Embassy, and was about to sigh, and walk away, when a man in a black suit appeared, as if from nowhere, and very hesitantly asked me what I wanted. It was as if he had been taken by surprise that a member of the public was standing in his hotel lobby. Perhaps it *was* unusual. Perhaps the hotel was only used by tour groups, and individuals just didn't come. Perhaps the hotel was closed for the winter. I will never know, but I could see that there were a few plastic sun beds at the edge of the pool, and I would have my choice. The place was deserted.

I explained that I would like a beer, and a swim, please.

Ah, yes, a swim would be ok, but not a beer. No alcohol here, but a coke could be found. My heart sank. I was weary. I was hot. I was tired, and needed refreshed in a nice swimming pool.

"Thank you, I'll have a coke then."

The pool was mine to do with as I pleased, since I seemed to be the only hotel resident, albeit temporary. I would not be the only resident of the pool however. On closer inspection, I discovered that lots and lots of other creatures were already frolicking in the cool waters. None of them were human, and most were pretty small. I hesitated, then, "What the hell!" and jumped in. God it was good. It seemed to wash away all the dust, and weariness, and anxiety of the last hours, and left me feeling exhilarated. I did make sure to keep my mouth shut though. I had no intention of having a second meal, just yet. In the depths of the hotel I could see two men, staring at me, and shaking their heads.

When I hauled myself out, checking that nothing strange had latched on to me, I couldn't bring myself to lounge on any of the empty sunbeds. It would have felt as if I was the only human left alive on Earth, except for the two aliens still watching me from the darkness of the reception. They were there as I dried myself on my tiny towel, but were nowhere to be seen as I left.

On the way back to the Niji I was fascinated to see a primary school disgorging its infants. Every one of them was immaculate in uniform, the girls wearing blue tartan dresses and the boys in blue blazers and black shorts. They would have put many British school kids to shame, and just as in Britain, their mums and dads were there to meet them, some even in cars. It seemed so incongruous in the middle of a rural African town with dust streets and sad looking concrete buildings, but I was to see this scene often as I travelled. Education, especially primary education, attracts a great deal of aid money, and some at least ends up as uniforms.

At the Niji, I made myself presentable and headed out to find the *Chez Frances* restaurant which my book recommended as one of the best in town. It apparently was only a hundred yards or so from my hotel, but could I find it? I walked up and down the street several times until I gave up and asked a local. He picked up on the "Chez Frances", and pointed to a tiny hand written sign propped against a tree just across the road. I had passed it twice without realising that this was the restaurant. It was, of course, in another of the unpretentious concrete blocks, but this one at least had once been painted a nice sky blue. It turned out that the restaurant was not actually *in* the building, but out the back. Here was a shady, dust-floored yard with a few big trees and some rather rickety tables and chairs. The food was produced through a hatch in the rear wall of the building, and brought to the table by an old man who could have been a waiter, but was more likely simply a helpful local. The main focal point was a huge television screen fixed to a wall, showing, of course, a football match being played out in some foreign land.

By now it was dark as I took a table near the back of the yard and ordered the omelette and chips which was becoming my staple diet. Looking round I could see, in the dim light, three Western faces, presumably French from their voices, and two young Africans, all engrossed in the game. It could have been almost any pub in Scotland on a Thursday night, except that this was Tambacounda in rural Senegal, I was outside in the warmth of an African evening, and the bugs were biting! It could easily have been Plockton!

When my omelette and chips arrived, it was delicious. 8 out of 10. (I had started giving scores). Monkey sat on the table beside me as we drank beer and watched football, with the call to prayer drifting over the roof and up to the myriad stars. I really did feel then that I was far from home, and alone.

Being very much aware that I would have another early start in the morning, I didn't linger too long, and headed back to the hotel for a last beer and bed. In Tambacounda there *are* street lights, but they don't work, so it was a dark walk. I was getting used to that.

In the otherwise empty hotel bar, I met Geordi, a Spanish guy from Barcelona who was *doing* Senegal, on his own. He was about my age, and we clicked. He seemed to be doing the same as me, but only in one country (no borders to cross). Since we could only converse in pidgin French, which neither of us was good at, it was hard going, but I did gather that he had been travelling by *taxi brousse* (bush taxi) all over Senegal for the last twenty days, and was due to fly home in another week. I never did find out why he was doing it. Maybe it was his birthday too! He was a very affable guy, and I would have been tempted to travel with him for a while, but Timbuktu beckoned, and I couldn't afford to get diverted.

In my bedroom I hung up my mosquito net from the handy hook above the bed, checked that my washing was drying nicely over a chair, slipped into my sleeping bag, set my alarm for 6.30 a.m. and crashed to sleep exhausted. It was about nine at night.

In the morning I was not going to be caught out again, so ordered breakfast *before* I left, and gorged myself on ham, cheese and as much bread as I could eat, all washed down with excellent coffee. That would have to last me for quite a while.

Now I was ready for the day, which, if successful, would see me over the border into Mali.

The Gare Routier was a fair distance away, so I took a yellow cab to get there and was relieved to find the place much smaller and a lot less frenetic than in Dakar. Luckily, there was a bush taxi waiting for a few more passengers before setting off for the border at Kidiri. My arrival meant that they only needed two more before setting off.

Michael arrived, sauntering up the road, with a big rucksac on his back, and a heavy looking, black *manbag* slung over his shoulder. In his bush hat and khaki clothes he looked like he knew what he was doing.

We introduced ourselves, and he told me that he too was travelling into Mali, to the Dogon region near to Timbuktu. He was about the same height and build as me, but was probably in his late thirties. I took to him, and thought that it might be good to have a travelling companion for at least a part of the way. He was French, but his English was good, and we were able to converse to a certain extent.

After about an hour, a last passenger arrived and we were able to leave at 9 o'clock. I had never crossed an African border before, and was a bit nervous, having heard stories of bribes, and corruption. I expressed these worries to Michael as we got into the taxi, and he stopped in his tracks, looked me in the eye, and said "Never give a bribe. NEVER!"

He seemed like he had a large bee in his bonnet but assured me that the taxi would take us over the border to a village on the other side called Diboli, and that he had done this kind of thing before. It would be easy. The taxi, a 504 of course, was comfortable enough, and with only 7 in it was not too crowded for a *short* journey of only 3 hours on a good tarmac road.

Kidira, on the Senegal side of the border, is small and basic, but is an important strategic point, being a transport hub on a main route east into Mali, and beyond. It sits beside the River Faleme, which marks the actual border.

I didn't have time to take in much of the details, since immediately we arrived at the Kidira Gare Routier, everyone got out, and we were told that the taxi would not cross the border! What now? I had no idea how to cross on foot, and what I would find on the other side if I did. All the Africans who had been in the taxi had gone their ways, and only Michael and I were left. Michael was in animated conversation with some drivers, and I could only stand and hope that some good would come out of it. I could barely follow French at such a rate. At this point I really thought I had bitten off more than I could chew. I couldn't speak the language. I was in the middle of a very foreign country, on my own, about to cross a border and carry on for another thousand miles. So what was to worry about?

Eventually the discussion stopped, and Michael told me that he had negotiated for us to be taken over the border by a different taxi, and that the delay was because he thought they were trying to rip us off, and had argued hard to reduce the price. I could only accept, and be grateful that I had an interpreter with me, in the shape of this likeable, but perhaps a little parsimonious, Frenchman.

We were quickly bundled into yet another 504, and driven at speed to the Senegalese border post, where without much ado, we had our passports stamped out of Senegal. Next, it was a dash across the border, with only the briefest of chances for me to take in the sight of my first big African river.

Although it wasn't the Niger, and was only a tributary to a much bigger one to the North, to me it was *big*. Perhaps this was only psychological, as it was the *border*, and a milestone on my journey. The fleeting glimpse I was afforded through the edge barriers of the bridge, showed me a 200 metre wide stretch of grey/blue water with steep sandy banks, dotted with a few very bushy green trees. In the distance, around the base of a railway bridge, a large group of people was gathered in and beside the water. Then I was past, and they were lost to sight.

4   TAKING A TRAIN

My first view of Mali was not encouraging. Where Kidira had been basic, it was at least, business-like. Dibola was just basic. We stopped at an old metal *customs* sign, propped up against one of the wooden shacks which lined the litter-strewn and very dusty main-street. Our driver took our money, then indicated that we should go to a shack about 30 metres away. He then sped off back to Senegal. Again I thanked the stars for my travelling companion, as although I was quite capable of getting my passport stamped, I had no idea what was to happen next. The driver had told Michael that another 504 would take us on to Kayes, a main Malian town about 3 hours' drive further east.

So, having successfully passed through *immigration,* which consisted of having our passports glanced at and stamped in a tiny room in one of the shacks, we wandered out into the street to look for our taxi. The street was simply an area of red dust, and where in Tambacounda the buildings were concrete boxes, here they were rough shacks of tarpaulin held up by wooden poles. While the whole scene looked temporary, it also looked as if it had been like that for ever. Captivating, but worrying, since there was no taxi to be seen, and certainly no sight of any building which might offer overnight accommodation.

There were a few people about, mainly loading pick-up trucks, and a couple of lorries came through, but as the time went on we realised that it was unlikely that any taxi was coming for us. Eventually Michael went back to the border post while I waited out in the street, marvelling at the array of goods that were being loaded on to the roof of what appeared to be a small lorry with a tin hut bolted on top of it. Bales of cloth, bundles of clothes, buckets, farming implements, a bicycle and kettles were piled up until the load on top was almost as high again as the shed. More goods were being loaded inside, along with people! I really couldn't see how, on roads such as were here, a vehicle loaded like this could last more than a couple of trips. As I watched even more being loaded, Michael returned, and pointed at the truck.

"That's our taxi."

He explained that the local name for such a thing is an "Alham", short for "Allah be praised", which everyone who travels in one says when they reach the end of their journey. It was going to Kayes, and was our only chance of getting there that day.

At least we had transport, and although I had again to rely on Michael to negotiate with the driver, which he did in his usual hard-bargaining way, I was beginning to really enjoy the challenge of travelling on a wing and a prayer.

We were told to take a seat inside the shed on the back of the truck, and looking in, I could see that it was going to be cosy, especially in the heat of the afternoon. The shed was approximately 2.5 metres by 3.5 metres, and once we were all loaded and ready to go, I counted 22 people inside, including myself, and we all had our luggage with us, along with what appeared to be provisions for a village shop. The metal roof sagged with the weight of the stuff on top, and I decided that if the whole thing collapsed, it would be better to be near the door. Seating was a row of seven people down each side, and one row of eight perched on a wooden board down the middle, held up by a couple of plastic buckets.

In the crush to get on, there was really little chance to choose where to sit, and Michael ended up on one side near the front, under an alarming bulge in the roof, while I was second from the door on the middle bench, albeit with a plastic bucket full of bottles severing my left leg, and a very large woman leaning on me, asleep on my right. I considered myself lucky.

There was a thin faced old woman in a green dress directly opposite me, which meant that, unavoidably, our knees were touching. This was quite embarrassing and more so when, even before we set off, she began a rant. Whether she objected to being so close to me, was feeling the heat, or was just out of sorts, I couldn't tell, but she went on, and on, and on, in a startlingly high shrill voice. Eventually others began to interject, and before we knew it, an almighty row had developed, with her screeching against everyone else and waving her arms about. Not a word of this was directed *at* me, but I had the impression it was *about* me. Michael was too far away for me to ask what was going on. Eventually everything quietened, but not before about ten of the passengers had, in unison, yelled "Shut up!" at the shrew. I was still left with knees locked to hers.

At this, I decided that perhaps I should try to ingratiate myself with my fellow passengers, and produced a little bag of sweets which I had bought in Dakar. There were a couple of young kids, and I offered a sweet to them. Their reaction was not what I expected. They shied away from me, and at the same time, the adults with them signalled to me that I should give *them* sweets. I thought that this seemed a bit forward, but happily shared with them, and with all the others who were now holding out their hands. Eventually, when all the adults, including the green woman, had taken a sweet, I handed one each to the kids. Their father promptly took the sweets from them and dropped them into his pocket. None of the adults had actually put a sweet in their mouth either. They had all squirrelled them away for later! *Ramadan!* I had been caught out again. It had taught me one thing though. If you are going to share, be prepared to share with *everyone*.

Eventually we were off, and it was then that I realised just how frightening this journey might be. With every dip or bump in the road, and the road seemed to be simply made of dips and bumps, the bulges in the roof sagged more, and the suspension groaned louder. I was convinced that we would all be crushed. It didn't happen, but within a mile we *were* stopped at a police check point, where all our IDs were checked, and a woman in black, Michael and myself were told to get off! Oh. Lord, what now?

The policeman motioned that we should follow him, and sauntered away very slowly with a swagger, towards his office, which was in a low concrete block. As we approached, I could see several more policemen, in faded green uniforms, sitting in a circle in some shade at the end of the block, laughing and eating pieces of melon. At the office, we were told to stand outside at a hatch, while the policeman went inside to the cool, then started to very slowly peruse our passports. The lady in black had been taken away elsewhere. It seemed that the procedure was taking much longer than necessary, and no words had yet been spoken, making me feel more and more nervous. I noticed that Michael had brought his bag with him, slung over his shoulder, and seemed to be holding it in a concerned sort of way. This puzzled me because we had both left our rucksacks on the truck where they would be vulnerable, and I wondered what must be in his small bag that made it so important. I was sure he would have his money safely in a body belt, and the cop already had his passport.

I started to worry, not so much that I might be about to have to pay my first bribe, but more that Michael, who was looking redder and redder by the minute, would explode, and get us flung in clink. I got my words in a second before Michael could start, and said in my broadest Scottish accent, "It's a great day isn't it? Is everything all right?" To my amazement, the cop broke into a big smile, said "Ecossais," and stamped our passports for the second time in Mali. He was beaming as he said a few words to Michael, who had thankfully returned to a normal colour, and then we were ushered to the end of the block where the picnic was taking place. None of the police there could speak English, but through Michael, and with a wee bit of French myself, I was able to answer most of their questions. I discovered from Michael that I had amazed them all that I was seventy one years old! When they had asked me my age, I had answered in French "I have sixty years," I thought, but actually I had said "I have sixty eleven." They reckoned that I looked wonderfully young for my age, and very adventurous for seventy one. Neither Michael nor I put them right, and I did wonder how closely the first one had checked my passport. How did he know I was Scottish? From my accent? Perhaps he wasn't so slow after all.

As we left them, I asked if they might sell me a piece of melon which looked so watery, cool and inviting in the heat. They refused, but gave a big piece to each of us for nothing. So, rather than having to pay the expected bribes, we were welcomed and given presents. Things were looking up.

While all this had been happening, our fellow passengers were waiting, sweltering in the shed on the truck, but none of them would have dreamt of complaining to the police! I was pleased to see that the lady in black was back on the bus as well, but as I clambered on, my little joke of shouting "Move right up the bus pleeeease." fell on deaf ears.

Again I was knees-locked with the green screecher, and for the next hour she sat and glared at me, while the large lady to my right continued to sleep against my arm. How she could sleep, being jostled mercilessly in a tin can in that heat, I do not know, but she even managed to snore. I made a good pillow.

Eventually, we stopped at the end of a track leading off into the scrubby desert, where a donkey and cart were waiting. Much to everyone's relief, this was the stop for the harpy in green, along with most of the gear inside the shed. I assumed that she was the keeper of a village shop somewhere nearby, and that this must be her weekly supplies. Everything was loaded on to the donkey cart, and the donkey promptly took off. On its own! There was huge hilarity inside the shed as we all craned to watch through the couple of little windows, while the woman, and a couple of men, took up the chase, yelling, and shouting at the beast to stop. Buckets, bags, and brooms started to cascade on to the dust from the runaway cart.

The mood within the group seemed to be *Serves her right!* and everyone was enjoying the spectacle, until it was realised that one of the men disappearing after the donkey was our driver. This meant that we might again be left roasting in the heat, and this time there was no shortage of men prepared to complain. The driver was shouted at, and told in no uncertain terms that he should be driving us to Kayes, not running round in circles after a donkey, especially *that* woman's donkey.

All this I gathered from Michael later. At the time, I just enjoyed being part of the whole thing.

Luckily, the central plank with its bucket legs was not part of the woman's load, and even luckier, the woman beside me decided to squeeze into the vacated place opposite me, giving me much more room to breathe, though restricting my legs even more. At least, she didn't seem to object.

The only other stop before we reached Kayes was when we eventually reached tarmac, and the driver got out to throw water on the wheels. By that time, I would have happily lain on the road and had him throw water on me too, but then I sneezed.

"I'm surely not getting a cold." I thought.

At 5.10 p.m. we reached Kayes, our destination for the night, and as I prised my bones out of that travelling tin can, I whispered, "Allah be praised!"

All our travelling companions soon disappeared in various directions, leaving Michael and myself to find our way to the *Hotel du Rail*, where we had both independently decided to stay the night. Since, from the guide book, the hotel appeared to be a couple of miles away, Michael suggested that we should share a local taxi. The taxi rank was a small area of rough ground and scrub across the road from the Gare Routier, where a few beaten up yellow cabs were parked, along with various groups of men, goats, and cattle. It looked more like a local farmers' market than a taxi rank. Michael again said that he would negotiate, and approached the first driver we saw. I tagged along like a pup, and as I expected, an argument arose. Eventually, Michael told me that the driver was asking for 1,000 CFAs for *each* of us, and that he was insisting that it should be 1,000 for the taxi. He decided to approach a different driver, but naturally word had got round, and none of the others would take him on. With lots of gesticulation and heated words, Michael broke away from the group of drivers, and told me that as they were trying to rip us off, and had now refused to take us at all, we should walk or wave down a driver on the road. For myself, I reckoned that although I didn't mind looking for a bargain now and then, there were times when one just had to pay the asking price, and have done with it.

A pound, come on.

I asked Michael to try to re-negotiate, as personally, I was happy to pay for both of us, if it would get us to the hotel, so he went back to them. He wasn't happy as he approached the group, and started to plead, with me at his side. As he was doing so, my attention became diverted by raised voices behind me, and I turned to see a large, brown, long-horned cow, which was tethered to a tree, pawing at the ground and looking me in the eye. The men with it were shouting at me and waving to tell me to run! It took a second to realise that although the beast was tied to the tree, it was tied by quite a long rope, and myself and Michael were just within its circle of influence.

Then it raced at us.

Being slightly forewarned, I was able to take enough quick steps backward to get beyond the horns, but I could see that Michael, engrossed in his negotiations was blissfully unaware of the situation, and the danger he was in.

I shouted "Michael! Look out!" just as he turned to see the point of one horn slicing towards him. He had no time to run, but whether by luck, or good judgement, he fell backwards on his backside and the horn passed within an inch of his head. A very quick and undignified scramble on his knees got him out of range of a second try, and he lay on the ground ashen-faced and gasping. He had been within a whisker of being gored.

All this happened in a flash, and at the end, the cow's keeper was just as pale as Michael, since having to compensate for the death of a Westerner would have been well beyond his means. I was also completely shaken as, although I hardly knew Michael, I could possibly have found myself responsible for his welfare, or repatriation of his body! Meanwhile, the taxi drivers were enjoying his predicament, and showing little sympathy. They did however agree to take us to the hotel, but still at 1,000 CFAs *each*. We paid, and then discovered that we were sharing with two locals, which made for an interesting little trip through the lesser travelled parts of the town, and was worth every penny, though Michael considered it to be adding insult to injury. He was lucky it was only his ego that was injured.

Kayes is a reasonable size at about 100,000 souls, and is certainly the centre of commerce for a huge area, but it is also very hot and dusty, and has few prosperous looking parts that we could see.

The Hotel du Rail is naturally, close to the railway station, and was chosen by me because of that, and because it appeared to be the only hotel in town. On the outside it had a very impressive edifice, and had the look and air of a small

Victorian spa hotel. It was quite pretty, and built of a light-coloured sandstone which glowed warm in the sun.

Inside it was dire. *Faded grandeur* would be too complimentary, and it was expensive at 17,000 CFAs for what they called a suite.

There were no towels, no toilet paper, no electricity and *no running water,* but there was soap! Although there was a shower, and there was a chance that the water might come on later, I decided that I couldn't wait to get the travel dust off me, so took a "kettle shower" using the multi-coloured plastic kettle, and bucket of water I found in the bathroom. It was a glorious sensation, and so unusual for me that I took a photo of myself mid-shower using the time delay on my camera. To spare any blushes later, it was a rear view.

Meanwhile, Michael had been out to check on trains to Bamako, and discovered that the next one would be the following evening. This allowed us a leisurely couple of beers in the spacious, but scrubby, hotel garden, followed by an expensive dinner of chicken and chips. The chips were ok, but the chicken, whose name I never learned, had been a weedy little chap, who deserved better.

Back in my room for the night, I lay on my bed, and let the day re-run through my head. I was too tired to attempt a night walk in Kayes to find an internet café, but it would have been great to tell Kate of the adventures of the day, and to describe my first impressions of Mali. I could conjure up the miles upon miles of flat scrub, and the villages of huts, not of straw or wicker, but mud, and looking desperately poor. I would have told her of the little baobab trees in the desert which looked as if they were growing upside-down, and which looked so pretty decked out in their bright pink blossoms. I also wanted to tell her of my surprise that I had a cold! I had always imagined that the common cold was a phenomenon of our Northern damp and dreich climate, and that although those who live in the tropics might enjoy the delights of yellow fever, malaria and dengue, they would hardly be troubled by a sniffly nose. Not so! As I sneezed and sneezed again, I remembered the young woman in the middle of my bush taxi out of Dakar, in whose company I had spent 9 hours. She had been coughing. She had a cold. Now I had it. Thinking more about this, I realised that I had indeed seen many small children in various places, with runny noses. It appeared that the common cold was a lot more common than I had imagined.

Another problem might be Michael. He was starting to talk in terms of "When *we* get to Mopti", which was on my route a few days hence. This suggested that he had decided to accompany me almost to Timbuktu, and would no doubt be intending to *look after* me. I didn't want that. This was *my* trip, and he had his. Perhaps I was becoming more confident, or just less grateful, but I felt that I would like to try making my own way, rather than with a guardian.

However, I liked the man, and he was interesting. He told me that he was a research engineer with a French oil company, but that he had decided to come to Africa for a spell to *do good works*. He was going to visit various charitable clinics in the same region as Timbuktu, and was carrying medicines for them, which he had funded himself. I wasn't able to work out whether these charities actually knew that he was heading their way, or if he simply intended to pitch up at their doors and say, "Hello, I've got drugs for you. Can I have a bed for the night?"

I did gather from him that this is actually often done by those travelling on the cheap, and if they offer to give a bit of help to the charity, they can get bed and board for little or nothing. He certainly didn't say that that was his intention, but did suggest that *helping charities* would give him the moral high ground in certain difficult situations, or so he thought. Although he didn't actually open it, he explained his concern regarding his manbag. This was where the drugs were! They weren't recreational drugs, he assured me, but medicines. However, a zealous border guard or policeman might make more than a little out of a bag full of drugs of any description, and it made me wonder why he seemed to take such a belligerent attitude to officials. He just explained that he hated even the hint of corruption. I had to agree with him, but recognized that one, at times, had to be pragmatic. Perhaps he could be a liability. I decided that we would part company in Bamako after the train journey and went to sleep sneezing, with a packet of hankies by my side.

A little incident in Kayes

The next morning, Saturday, Michael and I went off to the station to look for the train we would be on that night. As usual, there were a lot of young lads hanging about, who hassled us a bit, but Michael made it plain that they would get nothing from us, and anyway, we were just looking. When we got past them, on to the platform, there was a train standing alongside. It was a very old dusty green train, and looked so dilapidated it was interesting. Since all the doors were standing open, I suggested we pop on board and have a look. It appeared completely dilapidated, but still in service, so I took a photo of the inside of the carriage, to let Kate see later. It was dark enough inside for the automatic flash to fire. As we jumped off, and started to walk up the platform to get some outside shots, we heard shouting behind us, and looked round to see an old man in railway uniform beckoning us back. When we got to him, he started gabbling in fast French at me, and about half a dozen of the young men joined in. I assumed that Michael understood what was going on, and looked askance at him. Suddenly the boys grabbed me by the arms and started dragging me along the platform! I resisted and tried to shake them off, but they just pulled me harder, and in panic I thought "Jesus, I'm going to be mugged!"

Michael, white faced and still clutching his valuable bag, watched from a short distance away, but did not interfere.

I was hauled out on to the street, my heart racing. *What was going on?* With a huge effort, I broke free and got my back against the station wall, but they pounced on me, and holding even more tightly, started pulling me towards what appeared to be a semi-derelict building.

"God!" I thought, "This is the end of it, and Kate doesn't even know where I am."

I knew that retaliation would be pointless, and counter-productive, since one small sixty year old against six fit twenty year olds was no match, and Michael seemed paralysed. The only time I felt that I just had to react with violence was when I felt a hand sneak into one of my trouser pockets. I had no idea whose hand it was, but I did manage to get a grip of his wrist, and sank my nails in as far as possible. It withdrew, but I was panicked. Would they kill me? Surely not, but.... Visions of television pictures of machete attacks in other parts of Africa sprung up. They were hauling me across the street, and the expectation of being beaten up and robbed behind the building was making me hyperventilate. I struggled, and shouted out, "Help! Help!" There was no reaction except from some people sitting on a wall across the street. They laughed!

I shouted "Au secour! Au secour!" More laughter.

As a last resort, I shouted "POLICE!" That got a reaction. The lads who were accosting me stopped. They all started nodding, and pointed to the building, where I then could see a policeman, in green uniform, cap at an angle, relaxing on a chair in the sun.

It was the POLICE STATION!

Puzzled, but relieved, and still gasping for breath, I allowed myself to be dragged there, and when the boys released me with a push towards the policeman, I gratefully dodged round him and ran inside. Once we were all there, a hubbub got up with Michael, the policeman, the young touts, and the old railway man all speaking at the same time. The only one not talking was me. I was still trying to slow down the thumping of my heart to prevent the heart attack I was sure was imminent. Anyway, I had absolutely no idea what was going on. At one point, Michael leaned towards my ear, and whispered something to me. I don't know the French for "Delete the bloody photo of the train!" but I understood what needed doing, and just before the camera was demanded by the policeman, *dit,dit,dit* the photo was gone. Next, the passports were taken, both mine and Michael's, but luckily Michael's bag remained untouched.

So, no passports and no camera.

I wasn't sure which was more precious to me. I could replace the passport, but not the photos I had taken along the way. My mind went to bribes, and no matter what my travelling companion might say, I was prepared to use a bit of my budget to get my stuff back.

Once the policeman had calmed things down, and sent away the locals, he told us that he could not deal with this himself, and that we should come back in two hours, after morning prayers, when the *chief* would be there. This looked like it might be serious.

I was still in shock, and didn't have the presence of mind to try to sweet talk the cop, and anyway still wasn't sure what I had done wrong. As we left the police station, Michael confirmed what I suspected though. I had taken a photo of the train.

In Mali, that's a crime.

I got caught because the flash had gone off. The boys had seen the flash, and sniffed a *prize*. For them, this little incident would make their day.

Now, I was in a pickle. My passport was being held by a rural African policeman. The Chief of Police was no doubt going to accuse me of spying, and I hadn't reported in to *control* for two days. I had also involved Michael, and he had a bag of drugs.

I needed the internet.

I told Michael that I was going to try to find an internet café, and would be back in plenty time for the showdown.

In most towns, there are plenty of internet cafés, and I was sure that there would be one just up the street. I was wrong. Kayes would appear to be different. Eventually, after a futile search, I spent several minutes trying to make myself understood by a local. It seemed that she was telling me to go to the school where there was a computer. She pointed the way, and after threading my way through the narrow streets, I did discover what appeared to be a primary school. It was closed! A well-dressed woman in Western clothes, who could speak English, explained that since this was the last day of Ramadan, the school and most businesses were closed in preparation for a big celebration that night. There would be no internet until I got to Bamako. *Ramadan*! I had used up an hour in a futile search, and Kate still did not know of my predicament.

On the way to the hotel, I tried to work out what I would do if my passport was confiscated. Would I be fined? Would I be jailed? How long would I be in Mali? What about Michael and his drugs? I was going to hyperventilate again. And my cold was getting worse.

At the hotel, we decided that we should try to get tickets for the train, and asked the receptionist how we could go about this, as the station was definitely out of bounds for us for a while. He agreed to get them for us at 13,000 CFAs each for first class, and said he would have them for us after prayers. Everything was going to happen after prayers. Thinking of my forthcoming meeting with the police chief, I said a little prayer too.

At 10.15 a.m. we presented ourselves back at the police station, to find the original policeman still relaxing. Oh-so-slowly, he rose and told us to wait while he found the chief, who, after ten minutes arrived, not in uniform, but in a colourful flowing robe. We were ushered into a back room, where Michael immediately began to berate the man for the injustice of it all. I sat and played the *daft laddie* as usual, but tried very hard to keep up with the conversation. I could understand a lot of what Michael was saying, but virtually none of the replies. Eventually, the chief, who sat most of the time impassively, allowing Michael's rant to wash over him, indicated that I should go out and show the photos on my camera to the policeman at the door. The camera was produced from a drawer and I slowly clicked through all the photos, including of course, the last photo which was of my bare backside. However, there was no photo of any train to be found, thank God, and Michael (for the instruction to delete). The backside photo caused me a bit of embarrassment, and the lack of train caused the policeman some consternation! There was a hurried conversation between the cop and his boss, and the camera was placed on the boss's table.

"Show me."

Again I stepped through the photos, and he made me pause at various ones, though not at the last. No train. He looked puzzled, then a little angry, but said nothing, and just looked silently at the camera, which again lay on the desk. At this, Michael took his cue, and began berating him even more vigorously.

There is a book called "The Games People play," and one of the games is "Now I've got you, you son of a bitch!" Michael was playing this hard. Unfortunately, the chief held the cards, being our passports and my camera, and wasn't a man to lose face. That face was beginning to look more and more set against us, and I began to feel that Michael was overdoing things a bit. This could all go wrong.

I tapped him, indicated that I would like to speak, and in my best worst French, asked the chief if everything was ok, smiled my best smile and then asked if he had children. Without looking at me, he said "Two."

I had come prepared, and produced from my bag, two sparkly pencils, and two little polystyrene gliders, which I placed on the desk. Then, taking one glider out of its packet, I put it together, and holding it aloft, said I would like to give him a present for his children. He said not a word, and barely glanced at the toys, but slowly lifted our passports, inspected each one closely, then handed them to us, and the camera was slid across the desk to me. Phew!

Then, before Michael could say a word, I rose, took the chief's hand and shook it, while smiling and saying that it had been a pleasure to meet him, and please, could we go now? He waved us away. As we made our very relieved way back to the hotel, we could see, in the distance, the small group of young lads clustered round the entrance to the station, all looking in our direction. "Oh God," I thought, "I've still got to get past them again." and my blood ran cold despite the sweltering heat of the morning.

I did take on board the lesson learnt though. In Mali, don't take photos of trains, or if you do, *switch off the flash*.

After a couple of calming beers in the hotel garden, our nerves returned to normal, and things started to look up when the receptionist arrived with our train tickets. Had I doubted him? I was so relieved to get a ticket out of Kayes, that I gave him a big tip for his troubles. I would have kissed him if that had been appropriate.

Since the train wasn't leaving till about 8.00 p.m. Michael and I decided to walk up the street, and see the town. We noticed that a lot of the local kids were starting to come out on to the streets, dressed in their best clothes, and assumed that this was in preparation to celebrate the end of Ramadan. They all seemed well behaved and mannered, and many of them said "Bonjour" in passing, unlike my erstwhile friends at the station. It was great to feel relaxed again. I bought some food, including a tin of sardines, in preparation for the train trip.

Later I excused myself from Michael, and wandered on, still looking for an internet café. This proved to be useless, and I ended up sitting on a wall moping and drinking a Fanta in the middle of town, Ramadan or not. It then slowly dawned on me that the atmosphere in the town around me was starting to change. People were beginning to appear in groups, walking together and chatting, all in their *Sunday Best*. I could hear reggae style music drifting out from various side streets, and a carnival atmosphere was developing. It wasn't yet sunset, but there was only about an hour to go, and obviously tonight was going to be party night. I had almost a skip in my step as I headed back to the hotel. Ramadan was ending, I had not been beaten up or thrown in jail, and *I was soon leaving Kayes*.

We went to the station at about 6 o'clock, and the boys started to hassle us immediately. They wanted to know why we weren't in real trouble. "For what?" asked Michael. They *knew* I had taken a photo of the train, and couldn't understand how we had got away with it. There would probably be lots of accusations after we were away, but I didn't care, and was feeling almost brave now. They started to demand money, and as Michael weighed in verbally to them, I took from my rucksack a small bag of sweets I had bought in Dakar, and gave each lad a candy ball, telling them that that was all they were going to get from me. They weren't happy and still blocked our way on to the platform, so we retreated across the street and sat on a wall to wait till more passengers arrived. Safety in numbers.

A young French couple did appear soon after, and told us that they would be travelling to Bamako on the same train, but were off to have a meal first. This reminded me of my sardines and I made myself an impromptu picnic. It was delicious, but Michael didn't share with me. He was wise. Once we saw enough people heading into the station we made our move, and got through without any attention from the boys, who were working hard to earn tips. The train wasn't there yet, and the one I had photographed had disappeared. It hadn't, after all, been the one I would be on. All that for nothing! Och well, it would be a tale to tell my grandkids, some day.

The train arrived. Lo and behold, it was an old dusty green rattily affair, almost the *same* as the one which had given me so much bother. In fact it might have *been* the same one returned from hiding in a siding. Maybe it had been moved to stop me taking any more photos! Our first-class carriage was first class because most of the seats were intact. It was a big open carriage, and very dark since the lights were not on. I could just make out a few Malian passengers at the far end, while we whites took up position at the front. Soon the young French couple joined us, and we formed the Western enclave. It was comfortable enough, with each of us having a double, quite soft, green, mock-leather seat, but the lack of light could be a problem.

Michael's torch had just died, so since I was reasonably settled, I lent him mine.

At about 8.30 p.m. the lights came on, to a little cheer from the European contingent, and we were off. Goodbye Kayes.

Since it was dark outside, there was little to divert our attention, so I settled down with my own thoughts, while Michael and his compatriots chatted. I could tell that he was relating the tale of the photograph and *arrest*, sometimes to gasps, sometimes to giggles. I couldn't follow the whole conversation, but I did pick up one phrase from the French boy – "He'll never make it to Timbuktu on his own!"

"Oh yes I will," I thought. Young whippersnapper. That single comment convinced me that it would be time to split from Michael once we reached Bamako. I could tell already that he was starting to gravitate towards his new companions, who seemed to know their way around, and of course, spoke his language. They had come up from Bamako to Kayes, *just for the trip*, and I overheard them say that recently, bandits had held up a bus between Bamako and Kayes and robbed everyone.

I started to wonder how the hell I was going to get home!

The first few hours passed slowly, with the main diversion being the bugs flying up to the carriage lights which were very hot. These were not flies, nor were they moths as known in Scotland. These were huge, like small bats. Perhaps they *were* small bats, and as they hit the lights, they would be scorched, and fall with an audible *thud* on to the seats or floor, where they would crawl away to a dark place to recuperate before another suicide attempt. Fascinating as it was, I did wonder where they would land while we were asleep. The thought of waking to find a large angry hairy flying beast crawling across my face was enough to keep me sharp for a few hours. I didn't really mind. Thinking about my journey, both forward and backwards occupied me happily as we trundled through the night.

Every so often, the train would stop at some small village station, lit by fires in barrows, where women would throng outside the carriage windows shouting *"Pure Coffee, Pure Coffee,"* or *"Pombay, Pombay."* I saw young girls with torches, and buckets full of little plastic bags of water on their heads, and an old woman selling smoked fish from a basket. It was a surreal sight to see all this going on in the middle of the desert in the middle of the night, with the fire-barrows casting spectral flickering shadows across the scene. The train was a main outlet for these women's wares, and they desperately needed the trade. If you wished, you could open a window and buy a whole meal from the various sellers. (I did not wish). My sardine tea, mixed with an already dicky stomach, and the ever increasing effect of my cold was starting to incapacitate me. I needed a toilet! I hadn't investigated the rest of the train yet, since I had no wish to seek out any further excitement that day, and had kept quietly to my own little space in the carriage, but now I had to move, and quickly. I found that the nearest toilet was in the next carriage, and was a *sit-upon,* rather than a *squatty,* which was all good, but there the similarity with my toilet at home ceased. The pan was an open hole straight down to the rails, up which whooshed train noise, dust and a small gale. There was no toilet paper, no water, no towel, and no sink. I retreated to my carriage, and collected toilet roll, wet wipes, antiseptic gel, which my daughter had insisted I take at the last moment, my little towel, and a large bottle of water which I had hardly started. By the end of the operation, I had used half of most things, and almost all of my water, but at least I was at peace within myself, and felt clean. Rattling through the African night, being peppered with dust from behind, is a memory which stayed with me for a long time.

Sometime, somewhere in the night, as all was quiet and peaceful, my torch alarm went off! Everyone in the carriage was immediately awake. The screeching couldn't be ignored and an old African, half way up the carriage started to complain. I did nothing since I was waiting for Michael to switch it off. Michael did nothing since he didn't have it, he thought. I heard the French for "Switch that bloody thing off!" from various quarters, and asked Michael why he wasn't doing anything.

"You've got it."

"No I haven't. I gave it to you."

"I gave it back to you." In a slightly raised voice.

"Shut that bloody thing off!"

We were now both scrabbling in our bags to find the damned thing, each convinced that the other was to blame. We couldn't find it!

"*Weeeee, Weeeee, Weeee!*" it continued, until Michael gave a gasp, slapped his jacket pocket, and took out the torch, minus the pin.

"Oops, sorry."

I took the thing from him, opened a window, and hurled it into the night, still screeching and flashing. It arced far into the African darkness. I would like to think that the tale of that unidentified flying object is still told in some remote Malian village between Kayes and Bamako. Perhaps the poor little thing is lying in some dusty un-trodden corner, still giving an occasional weak "phweek", hoping to be rescued from its fate.

We got to Kita just before sunrise, and stopped for prayers. By this time, I think we were all praying for the journey to be over, but there were still five hours to go!

Just before we moved on, a huge container train passed us, heading up country. I had never seen a train like that. It was like a high, continuous grey steel wall which went on for miles. I wondered where so many goods could be going in Mali, and who could buy them, but then realised that it was probably all being shipped out through Dakar.

The rest of the journey was fairly bland, with only the occasional mud-hut village to break up the never ending scrub, and since the bugs had disappeared into their lairs as light returned, I managed to snatch a few hours' fitful sleep without fear of being cuddled by one. At about half past eleven in the morning after about fifteen hours travel, we pulled in to Bamako station.

5. BAMAKO

As I stepped on to the platform, my heart sank. Where there had been half a dozen young touts in Kayes, here there was a sea of them, all jostling one another to get to the passengers. I could feel panic rising as they came towards me, and was tempted to take up Michael's offer to accompany him and the French couple to the Lebanese Mission where there was cheap accommodation, but I stuck to my resolve, to go it alone, and managed to thread my way out on to the street for a taxi, with a multitude of "Non, merci."s and luckily no one grabbed me or pulled at me, so I didn't even have to scream for help.

I had explained to Michael before we arrived that I had decided to travel on under my own steam, and with a doubtful look on his face, we exchanged names, addresses and good wishes. He was intending to travel with the young couple. We promised to keep in touch.

I had already ear-marked the Colbris Hotel where I fancied spending a couple of nights. It was near the river and seemed to be fairly up-market. I felt I could do with a little bit of luxury.

It was not to be.

Firstly, the hotel was well away from the centre of town, which would not have been handy, and secondly it was full! So, after a fifteen hour almost sleepless train journey, I decided to *walk* the two or three miles uphill back towards the station, to my second choice hotel, Les Cedres.

Yes, a glutton for punishment.

Actually, it was quite an appealing prospect, since it was, as usual, a really nice day and in such a new vibrant place I was really in no great hurry. As I left the hotel area and headed towards the river bridge, I realised that this part of

Bamako was not exactly salubrious, and a lone, old, tired looking white man with a little rucksack on his back, walking through the middle, was attracting some attention. Yet again, I became aware of being followed, this time by two hungry looking young guys. I was too weary to dodge, and they could easily have stripped me clean. I doubt if anyone would have objected, so – "TAXI!"

Driving back up through the town, I could see that Bamako was different from Dakar. Where Dakar was cosmopolitan, Bamako was much more parochial, although it had its fair share of big new commercial buildings. Again, most people were walking, and there was a feeling of "market town" about it, even though it was the country's capital with about two million people.

Les Cedres Hotel consisted of a couple of low white buildings like small barns, with outbuildings at the back. However, it had rooms, and I was tired, and needing a good wash. To find that my room, in the outbuildings, was huge, with three beds, a working shower, and air conditioning came as a great, and very welcome surprise.

A cool shower, with real water, was such a luxury, and left me refreshed and ready to explore. First though, I had to do my washing, and ironing (lay things on bed, and pat them flat) so that I would look presentable enough to ask to use the internet at a posh hotel down the road. The guide book said that this was possible, but a bit expensive. Hang the expense! I wanted to contact Kate.

On the way out, I took in the *public* area of the hotel. This was a big open-air bar/restaurant, with some fairly modern tubular chairs, like you would see in a village hall in Scotland, and some tables covered in rather nice patterned table cloths. There was a higher level, next to the main building, under a car-porch style roof. The main section, in the open, was divided from the road by a high white wall sporting a few large electric lanterns. A group of white tourists were eating on the upper level, and appeared to be enjoying a good meal. Although the whole place had a rather run-down look and was far from upmarket, I was beginning to acclimatise, and reckoned that it would do for a day or two.

In my freshly washed and "pressed" tee shirt and trousers, I sought out The Grand Hotel, Bamako. Now this was a different kettle of fish. This was European standard. Plush tiled entrance hall, real reception desk, a porter, uniforms, and with relief I saw a bank of three computer points. The receptionist was most helpful and in perfect English, she told me I could certainly use the internet for as long as I liked, for a cost. Yes, the internet was working, and I could use booth number three. Joy.

The keyboard, of course, was of the WEIRDY type, so it took me more than an hour to do a page of up-date. The story of my fracas in Kayes featured heavily, as it still did in my mind, but I also had to tell Kate how much I was missing her, which I was. Then, since there was no immediate reply, I decided to wander the streets a little, on the way back to Les Cedres for a meal. I arranged to return to The Grand later, to check for Kate's reply.

Almost immediately outside the hotel, a group of young kids started cat-calling me, and spitting on the ground near me. I wasn't sure if this was personal and I had an unlikeable face, or because I was white. Either way, I felt an air of threat, and in my still fragile state, after Kayes, it was pretty unsettling. It certainly seemed to me so far that Mali was not quite as friendly as Senegal. I hoped that things would improve further East. Perhaps being tired, having a cold and a dodgy stomach was influencing my view.

I scurried back to Les Cedres, and ordered Spag Boll and a bottle of Flag (to settle my stomach). The white family was still there, but seemed a bit stand-offish, so I sat alone, on the open lower level, and at ease - until *The Honourable Bullo Kompte, Director General of the Cabinet of General Things* arrived. He was a very large, colourfully dressed African guy, who appeared through the gate from the road, and came straight up to my table, shook my hand, introduced himself, and sat down.

He (he said) was very high up in the Mali government, and could be of great help to me, and unfortunately his car had broken down - and he had no money with him.

Now, since Kayes, I had a very healthy respect for anyone who might even slightly represent authority in any way, and here was a grand government official (he even wrote his title down in my little notebook) obviously needing cash and help.

All my French left me. I could hardly remember a word, so of course, if I couldn't understand him, I couldn't really help him. It was unfortunate, but I bought him a beer, and after downing it pretty quickly, and without even glancing at the others in the restaurant, he left, telling me that he would return to meet me again the next day. I hoped not.

After hiding in my room for a while, I made my way back to The Grand to see if I had any emails. In the dark, I walked quickly along the quiet streets. There were some street lights here, and no rough sleepers, so I relaxed a little. At the Grand there was an e-mail from Kate and it was really uplifting to know that she was there, and not only knew exactly where I was, but probably knew more about Bamako than I did. She was obviously worried about me, and suggested that I could maybe find an organised tour group to join for a few days' respite. That would probably have been a good idea, but I had my itinerary now worked out, and I reckoned that with a decent sleep that night, I would cope.

She also told me that she had read on the web that if I was going to be travelling to Timbuktu down the Niger, by pinasse, I should get myself a foam mattress to lie on. Otherwise I would find myself probably lying on corrugated iron, cold and sore. She said that she had read that I would be able to buy one in Mopti. Obviously *NASA CONTROL* was doing my research for me.

It all turned out to be good advice.

I sent her a little "night night" message, and promised to e-mail again the next day.

Back at Les Cedres, I hung up my mosquito net over a bed, spread my silk sleeping bag out, climbed in, and was asleep before I knew it.

Over breakfast the following morning (Monday 15th Nov) I met Steve, a Londoner of indeterminate origin. He was at a table with Amsala, his *guide,* and Idrissa, a local taxi driver. Steve was probably in his fifties, bald with a goatee beard and a very sallow complexion. He also had a travel bag made out of what appeared to be a whole pig, minus the head! He seemed a bit of a wide boy, and explained that he was based in Mopti, but was here in Bamako to send some *bits and pieces* back by air to London. The impression given was that these bits and pieces should not really be leaving the country, but since he knew someone at the airport, it would be ok. I was fascinated, but not completely convinced that he wasn't spinning me a yarn. When he heard that I would be travelling by bus to Segou, then Mopti, he suggested that I should go with him and his guide in the taxi to the airport, and then to the bus station to buy my ticket for the next day.

I had to make a judgement on this, since there was the obvious chance that Steve really was doing something a bit dodgy, and we would all be picked up and hauled off to the police (Oh no, not again), but it was an offer of transport, and company to the bus station, which might be an intimidating place, if the train station was anything to go by. So I agreed to join them.

At the airport, Steve led us into a modern porta-cabin-type cargo office, where he had a quiet discussion with an official he seemed to know, and then his large parcel was handed over. The conversation was fast and in French, and I couldn't make out if all was legitimate or not, so I was glad to get out of there and back into the taxi. The taxi driver, Idrissa, and I had exchanged a few words while Steve was busy, and I found him a likeable guy, whom I thought I could trust. I had reservations about Amsala, however, who said little.

At the bus station, I realised I had made a good decision to go with Steve and Idrissa. As we approached, a crowd of really aggressive young touts swarmed all around the taxi, with their hands and arms in through the open windows. They were yelling at us, their faces inches from ours, and clung to the car, even as it accelerated. Idrissa told us to shut all the windows, and stay inside while he went and bought my ticket to Segou. I sat back, thankful for his help, while he, being used to this kind of situation, simply strode through the crowd, pushing them to the side as he went. He was of no interest to them, but they continued to shout at us through the windows. Idrissa soon returned with my ticket and once I had paid him, we sped off back to the hotel, where I arranged with him to pick me up early the next day to take me to the bus. It was good to think I would have a friendly face to help me through the melee. Before they left, I bought beers all round, and promised to meet up with Steve again when I got to Mopti. He told me he would be at *Le Campement Hotel,* which was where I intended staying too.

Now on my own again, I decided to spend the afternoon emailing then wandering in downtown Bamako. Part of me said that I should play safe, and stick to the hotel, but it would have been wrong to come this far and not see a little of the city. It would probably be worthwhile since I would be coming back this way on my return.

At the Grand Hotel, it was great to find messages from Kate, and my daughters, but it was difficult to carry on a conversation by e-mail, so I decided that at some time in the journey, I would try to phone home, maybe from Mopti. On the way out from the hotel, the receptionist told me that they were just completing an annex where the cost of the rooms would be much less than in the main building. It would be open by the time I returned. This was a ray of hope, since the price was not much more than the cost of a room at Les Cedres, but the facilities were *so* much better, *and there was a swimming pool*!

It wasn't very far to the main hubbub of Bamako, but on the way I began to feel pretty rotten, and amazingly weak and shaky. Although by now my cold had become a real streamer, and was enough to make me miserable, this seemed something more, and I was beginning to break out in a cold sweat.

I realised that I was having one of my *turns,* and needed to get somewhere cool to sit down. Although I didn't know it at that time, I suffered from hypoglycaemia, where my blood sugar level would suddenly drop, and I would feel *weird* as I would put it. Normally, if I simply sat, or lay down for a couple of hours, I would come round, after a bit of shivering, and complaining. Kate would usually bring me a cup of tea and a biscuit or two, and I would slowly improve. But I was in a main street in Bamako with no soft couch to lie on. I was really hungry, and felt that that was maybe causing me to feel so bad, so I got myself to *Le Rayoume de Gourmands* patisserie, as quickly as possible. I had been told that this was one of the best places to eat in Bamako, and that it was clean and modern.

It certainly was, though the service didn't come up to the same standard. Sitting in this beautifully cool and stylish restaurant, I was out of the bustle and hassle of the street, but could still enjoy the view of all that was going on through the huge plate glass windows. Unfortunately, though, I was in desperate need of food and comfort, both of which seemed to be in short supply. Luckily, an omelette appeared before I passed out, and a fair while later it was joined by some chips. The taste of the meal deserved a ten, but the service reduced the score to a five. Pity.

At least I was sitting and I was cool, as the street outside sweltered in the afternoon sun. I slowly recovered from what had been a *hypo*, and eventually ventured, a little shakily, back out in to the real world. Stepping out of the door was like stepping into an oven – a very busy, noisy, and hot oven. I headed up the Boulevard du Peuple to see the market, and was immersed in the sights and sounds of the place. It was a melee of green mini buses, whistling touts, girls with baskets of everything on their heads, swarthy Tuaregs in flowing clothes, stalls of shoes hats and gloves, torches on boxes, crates of chickens, fish on stalls and on the ground, people washing clothes in tubs on the pavement, and cops in green uniforms, with truncheons and loud whistles. My head could hardly take in everything that was happening around me, and I forgot my inherent fear of being "attacked". I plunged in.

Normally I carry with me at all times, a tiny Swiss Army Knife, which comes in handy more often than one might imagine, but it had of course been confiscated at Aberdeen airport, and I now felt naked. I was sure that there would be a stall where I could get a replacement, and it didn't take long to find one. Unfortunately, the knives on display seemed to be mostly of the machete variety, and I wasn't intending to hack my way through the jungle (I hoped), or start an insurrection. All I wanted was a little knife to cut string or Elastoplast, hopefully with a pair of tweezers, and a tooth pick thrown in. On that stall in Bamako they do not sell Swiss Army Knives. The smallest knife I could find was a *flick knife* with a four inch blade, which would have had me charged within minutes in Britain.

I bought it without asking if it was legal to carry a flick knife in Mali.

On my way out of the market I noticed several of the Tuaregs were openly carrying rather long curved knives in sheaths at their waists. Oh well, if it's all right for a Tuareg, it should be all right for me.

Here in Bamako was where I first saw the Tuareg. These, mostly nomadic, tribesmen were striking in their indigo blue turbans, which many of them wound over their faces as well as their heads, leaving only their eyes clear. They stood out in Bamako, among the young jeans-clad modern kids, and the business-suited workers. They were certainly in a minority, and would have looked more in place on the back of a camel, than on the streets of a city.

Now, feeling much better, and fully equipped with my new knife (the size and weight of which I was acutely aware) in my pocket, I decided to check out the tourist office, which was a short walk down towards the river.

Being the capital city, Bamako's tourist office is a government department, although a rather laid back one. Here I met Mr Issa Camara, who at least appeared to be the genuine article (as opposed to my erstwhile "friend", the Honourable Bullo Kompte), and he told me that *express* trains ran from Bamako to Dakar every Wednesday and Saturday at 7.00 a.m. and that a plane flew every Tuesday. All this was subject to *availability* which I took to mean *if it's running*. Since I had no idea when (or maybe even, if) I would be coming back through Bamako, I couldn't book anything, so just filed the information away in my head - and, of course, promptly forgot it. He also suggested that when in Timbuktu, I should contact a Mr. Bastos, who was his friend, and who would be able to help me. According to him, Mr Bastos was *Mr Big* in Timbuktu. I thanked him and assured him that I would certainly look up his friend.

Now, since I was beginning to flag again, it was time to head back to my hotel. On the way, I stocked up with lots of paper hankies, since again my nose was streaming.

It was a bit surreal that evening to find myself eating steak and chips, drinking beer and watching *Crouching Tiger, Hidden Dragon* on television in the open air, in Bamako.

Since Idrissa, the taxi driver, would be coming for me at 7.15 a.m. I paid my hotel bill before going to bed. I was still feeling poorly with *man flu,* however cheered myself up by winding up my little monkey chum, and watching him chitter sideways across the tiled floor. Such was I reduced to.

6. BAMAKO TO MOPTI

The alarm on my watch wrenched me out of heaven at 6.00 a.m. while it was still dark. It hadn't been a good night. My cold was getting worse, and I was nervous that I'd sleep in, so, for most of the night I kept waking up and looking at the time. At about 5.00 a.m. I had finally fallen into a lovely deep sleep. *For one hour.*

It was already warm as I packed, then quietly made my way round to the café, where a light was on, and someone going about.

"Great". I thought, and asked for a coffee and some bread.

"Sorry, there is none."

So, a nice bottle of cool water was breakfast. Great indeed.

Sitting alone at a table out in the open, waiting for Idrissa, I felt nervous. I wished that I didn't get so agitated about the touts at the stations, and realised that if Kate was there for me to *look after,* then I would be a lot braver, but she wasn't there, and I missed her. A lot.

I was beginning to feel miserable because I seemed to be always feeling miserable, and hoped that Segou, my next stop, would be restful and raise my spirits. It seemed sensible, after so many early starts and long journeys to just do this *short* hop to Segou which was only four hours away, rather than head all the way to Mopti in one day, which would have been another nine hour trip. I pushed to the back of my mind the fact that I had read, before I left Scotland, that there had recently been an outbreak of cholera in Segou. I would be fine.

Idrissa turned out to be perfectly dependable, and in gratitude I gave him some of my little stock of toys for his kids, when he arrived at 7.15 a.m. As we approached the bus station, he reminded me to close the window on my side, but at that early hour, the frenzy of touts hadn't really started in earnest. Once we had stopped, and I had paid him, he led me through to the bus and saw me on. I felt like an old man being helped across the street, but was very grateful to him. With him beside me the touts kept clear, as he made it plain that I was *his* charge, and they weren't welcome. He explained to me that I shouldn't really be too intimidated by the young lads, who really only wanted about 100 CFAs for *helping*. It was probably their only means of income, and they were desperate to take something home to their families each day. They might even be the only bread winner. He suggested that next time I should single out one of the lads to be my helper, and that would ensure that the rest would leave me in peace. From the way he spoke, I guessed that once, in his youth, he had plied the bus station himself. I thanked him for the advice, and promised myself that I would do as he suggested if I had the nerve.

I made sure that I got Idrissa's name and number written down in my notebook for future reference, then found a seat to myself near the back of the bus. It was bliss to settle in, and look forward to four hours of rest.

My fellow passengers were an eclectic bunch, ranging from Tuaregs in turbans, to large *mamas* in wonderful bright coloured dresses, to wiry old goatherds in traditional dress including daggers and God knows what else, to young moderns in tee shirts, with mobile phones. It amazed me, the number of people I saw with mobile phones. This was one of the poorest nations in Africa, and they all seemed to have technology that I barely knew how to use.

The bus which was comfy, had air conditioning and piped music (African), and I was able to spread myself a bit and relax. At little bus stops, girls came on with trays of glasses of tea, water and food, so I was able to have my breakfast as we went along. This was getting better all the time and since there was little of interest to see, except for scrub and the occasional mud hut village, I dozed on and off. One little detail I did notice and which stuck in my mind, was the big clay ovens in the villages, built a bit like old fashioned beehives, but with the rim of a lorry tyre as the door. Nothing was wasted.

As the bus was carrying on to Mopti, I was dropped off on the main road just at the entrance to Segou and was surprised to see that I was on a tarmacked dual carriageway, complete with street lights! Needless to say, someone appeared pretty quickly to help me, and got me a taxi to the Auberge Hotel. I gave him 500 CFAs, for which he seemed pretty grateful. One tout, I could handle. Or maybe he was just a guy being helpful.

Segou is a tourist destination, and so the hotels cater for their tastes. The Auberge was *Heaven*, and wouldn't have been out of place on the Med. It was small, and painted in the same orangey pink that the Oceanic had been (Oh so long ago!). Best of all, it had a shady back area with a very clean, tiled swimming pool, where I ordered a beer, and sat in glorious isolated splendour. There was only me, and 2,000 geckos. These little green friendly lizards were everywhere, running, jumping, mating, but thankfully not swimming. This was just what I needed – a bit of R and R. I swam, in an island pool, surrounded by a sea of geckos, then lay back and baked in the sun. OK, this wasn't *Africa,* but I could take it. Who knows, maybe my bloody cold would lift!

My allocated room wasn't in the main building of the hotel, but in an annex across the road. This was probably because I didn't appear to be the same calibre of tourist as they were used to. It was fine, though. A cool, clean, green-painted room, with a cool, clean bed and en-suite facilities. I could have happily ended my trip there, but of course, a little voice told me that I should make the best of it, as tomorrow I was off again to Tim! Perhaps it was the monkey speaking.

I decided to explore, and wandered out into the street, down towards the river. There were touts here too, but they were different from the station ones. These were *tourist touts* and were almost polite. Their job was to lure people into the few little tat shops which ran down the opposite side of the street. I assured them all that I would buy something once I had seen everything on offer, and they smiled and wished me a good day. I couldn't believe just how friendly, and calm things were here.

I wandered lazily downhill and at the river, I got my first real look at the Niger. I was able to stand and stare, without feeling nervous, and when I asked two old men on the ferry pier if it would be ok to take photos of the folk going about their business in and at the water, they looked at me quizzically, and said "Of course. Why not?"

Why not indeed, but they hadn't been with me in Kayes.

It was so pleasant to stand in a cool breeze and drink in all that was happening. This part of the river had sandy banks where huge long working pinasses were drawn up. Some were loaded with wood, gathered from the water, some with grass harvested on the far shore, and destined for cattle feed and others with goods for outlying villages. On the banks, women washed their clothes while kids jumped in beside them from the side of the ferry. Men drove donkey carts along the riverside, picking up wood and goods as they went. This was normal everyday activity here, and although the people looked far from prosperous, they appeared content, and I heard a lot of laughter. I saw no sign of the cholera that had worried me before I left Scotland. Feeling hungry, I reluctantly left the river, and found the Soleil du Minuit restaurant in the middle of the town. This was a tiny place with tables at the edge of the street, where I had, of course, an omelette and chips, which certainly rated a nine out of ten. At that time of day, it was quiet, and I could relax. There were a few white tourists around, some eating near me, but I didn't feel like talking, just relaxing. Later, I decided to email Kate from a hotel nearby, and discovered that she was sitting by the computer at home. That was great because we were able to spend more than 30 minutes *chatting* back and forward. I got emotional, and almost asked her to come out and meet me in Dakar on the way back, but ended up by suggesting that we should toast each other with a glass of wine at exactly the same time at 8.00 p.m. that night. Then I was drawn back to the river, and just sat for a while, enjoying the cool breeze. There was a little restaurant, the Esplanade, with a narrow riverside terrace there, and I decided that it was the perfect place for that glass of wine with Kate later.

It was a *good* day, perhaps the first since I had arrived in Africa that I could say I felt relaxed and happy with the trip. I was really enjoying myself, and wandered down to the nearby Bozo fishing village. All along the banks of this wide, placid river women were washing clothes, utensils, babies and themselves. It was so tempting to take photo after photo, but I didn't – not from fear of being hauled off to the police, but because I didn't want to break the spell. It was simply good to walk among them. The village itself was a mixture of mud and wooden huts, with long pinasses hauled up on the river bank. The bozo people are the masters of the water.

Walking back towards my hotel, I stopped at a tiny hardware shop and bought two little goat bells to take home. These were my first souvenirs, and although they were far too heavy for carrying hundreds of miles, I just had to have them.

Although I realised that there was more than a little "catch the tourist" about them, it was still interesting to browse the *on the street, on the ground* stalls, selling everything from pots and pans to water melons. The owners, mostly large colourfully dressed women, were happy for me to take their photo with their goods spread out before them – for a small donation.

I allowed one guide to lure me into a souvenir shop where I bought a little metal lady, but decided that that was the last souvenir for now.

Back on the terrace of the Auberge, with a cool beer in hand, I admired the way a couple of young touts worked the few tourists up and down the street. They were enthusiastic, and really quite good. Their *modus operandi* was simple - spot a likely tourist, walk beside them, befriend them, then divert them into the target shop. They seemed to work for all the shops, and probably got a commission on any sale. Since Segou obviously depended on tourists being happy, there was thankfully no air of threat.

Chatting with a few of the other guests on the terrace, I gathered that the Dogon region was very interesting, but Timbuktu was "nothing much". They suggested that I should see both, but I knew that would be impossible. "nothing much" or not, I was going to Timbuktu, and was sure that my view of the place would be different from theirs. It appeared that Segou was a setting off point for groups of about a dozen tourists who were transported in comfort to Timbuktu by road and posh pinasse for a night. All was laid on, and I reckoned that they would see very little of the real thing. I was doing it the hard, but more interesting way. I was a *Traveller*.

Soon it was time to go and *meet* Kate at the Esplanade. On closer inspection, I decided not to eat there, and bought a beer for our little drink together, since there apparently was no wine. The atmosphere wasn't quite what I had hoped for. There were only two others in the place – a large, loud, and continually grunting American man, who appeared to have escaped from a tour group, and a fairly young, very disabled

African guy, who could only get around by sliding himself on his backside like a baby, which made me feel guilty. The American aggravated me with his complaining and grunting and the African kept hassling me for cash, which he got. I retreated to the far end of the little concrete terrace and at exactly eight o'clock, raised my glass. In my mind I clinked it with my wife's, far away in Scotland, but at that moment, so near.

Since this was not my favourite place, I fled to the Soleil du Minuit, and had the best meal of the trip so far; *Capitaine Barbeque* with boiled spiced potatoes. Capitaine is a Niger fish caught nearby, so this was the local equivalent of Haddock 'n' Chips, but beautifully served and delicious.

As I had the prospect of yet another early start and long journey by bus to Mopti the next day, bed was beckoning.

The call to prayer had me awake at 4.30 a.m. but I lay for a couple of hours dozing on and off and trying to convince myself that I really wanted to get up and do another hard day's travelling, nursing an accursed cold, which was really starting to affect my mood. Eventually I rose, packed, and headed down to the river. My spirits lifted in the calm morning air. There was quiet activity by the river, where women were collecting multi coloured buckets of water, and the men were preparing their stalls. There were a couple of sailboats out on the placid surface of the Niger, and the low far bank was just visible through the early morning haze. I could have stayed there forever, but a bus beckoned, and in Mali, if you miss a bus, there might not be another one for a very long time. I headed to the bus station, receiving quite a few smiles and "Bonjours" on the way. I really liked this place.

When I arrived, I found it was a *regular* bus station like you would find in many small towns anywhere in the world and there were no touts. Oh joy.

The system seemed to be that when you bought a ticket, you gave your name to the clerk, who wrote it on a list. Once the bus was ready to leave, he would call the names in order, and you would choose from whatever seats were left. It was a bit like Easyjet, but less chaotic.

Since the bus wasn't leaving till 9.00 a.m. I was early, and so, quite well placed on the list. With time to spare, I bought some breakfast from a stall and settled down on one of the rows of open-air benches to enjoy waiting for a bus in Africa. I was the only white face there for a while, and I started to relish that situation. The slight frisson of threat, and differentness, gave me a small insight into what it must be like to be the only *black* face somewhere else.

The bus station appeared to be a remnant of an old colonial age, and had been allowed to deteriorate a bit. There was a goat tethered to a stanchion of the waiting-shed, next to a couple of mopeds, and two wee boys begging for their breakfast. I gave them a little of my bread before they were sent scurrying away by the old guy with the big stick, who was *security*. It seemed that begging and hawking were not allowed, but when a little girl led her blind mother into our midst, and they started to sing, the place went silent. Perhaps it was because I had been travelling for so long, but I thought that I had never heard such beautiful music. It almost made me cry, and I gave them more money than I should have. The mood was soon broken when a vast woman arrived with her many kids, all shouting and bawling and fighting like kids anywhere. I reckoned it was going to be a noisy trip.

While I watched, two white women appeared, and simply jumped on to the bus and sat on the best seats at the front. The security man with the stick was quick to tell them to get off, buy their tickets at the office, and take their turn in the queue. As they quietly got off the bus, I wondered that these two well-built women who looked as if they were seasoned travellers, with cropped hair and dusty clothes, didn't know the ticket system. Then I noticed that they had left some of their bags on the seats. They knew the system very well. When names were called and people filed on in the correct order, nobody liked to move the bags, and so, when it was their turn, they simply returned to the best seats.

When "Mister Djo" was called, I took a seat mid bus and we eventually set off at 9.45 a.m. with African music blaring from the loudspeakers, and kids screeching. Fifteen minutes later we stopped for a moped to be hauled up on to the roof, and folk got off to buy food and drink. One young man who was across the aisle from me returned with a vegetable which looked a bit like a hard leek. He offered me some which tasted like raw turnip, but not as appetising. This was his morning snack. There was no air conditioning on this bus and it was beginning to get very hot. The continual African music was starting to wear my brain down, and occasionally, I started to *think* I could pick up snatches of English being spoken around me, and then, more worryingly, *Gaelic. I don't speak Gaelic*. Luckily, at about 1.00 p.m. we stopped for prayers and I was able to get off to stretch my legs and buy some lunch. This consisted of a couple of meat sticks, like thin kebabs, a large water and a coke. It wasn't omelette and chips.

Further on, at a wayside stop, a large group of very wild looking men got on. They were wearing a huge variety of what appeared to be outlandish costumes, but were actually simply in their day clothes. There were plenty of knives and short curved swords in evidence. I assumed that they were local herdsmen, but since language was an impermeable barrier, I never discovered their story. They certainly quietened the kids!

One of these wonderful old men sat down next to me, so I was a bit tight for space, and since the bus was again sweltering with no windows open, and the music was blaring even louder, I was starting to hear the Gaelic again. I was feeling really miserable, with my streaming cold, tiredness, hunger, and the never ending music.

Then a wonderful thing happened. The music died away for a moment and when it came back it was Celine Dion gently singing *our song* – "My heart will go on".

As I realised what I was hearing, something burst inside me, and a flood of hot tears poured from my eyes. I could have wiped them away, but didn't. I let them flow, stinging down my face, down my neck and on to soak my shirt. I sat staring, but not seeing, straight forward and let it happen while the old goatherd beside me simply didn't notice. I think perhaps he understood, and allowed me to have my time.

For three minutes I was in another world.

I know it wasn't a hallucination, since the song played right through to the end, and then the African music resumed, but I wondered if somehow, just somehow, Kate had caused that song to be played on that bus at that time at that place in Africa, because she knew I was low. I think so.

The rest of the journey passed in a bit of a daze, with no other Western songs and I managed a nod to the understanding old man as he left at his village. He said a word or two to me which I only understood from his eyes, and I smiled a small embarrassed smile in return.

After a seven hour journey, we eventually pulled in to Mopti. I was glad.

Mopti was as I had imagined it from other travellers, and from my guide book, a vibrant transport hub on the Niger, and also a main centre for tour groups heading to the Dogon region and Timbuktu. That's not to say that it was in any way sophisticated. Mopti is a typical mid African town with red dust roads, ramshackle buildings and apparent chaos. There are, however, some nice places, like the Kanaga Hotel, which is, for the area, posh and cosmopolitan – and expensive. I didn't go there - couldn't afford it, but headed straight to *Le*

Campement Hotel which was within my budget. In fact, it should have been within everyone's budget. The electricity was off, the water was off, and the manager smelled of whisky! But I was tired, and I wouldn't be staying there long, so I signed in.

My first room I had to abandon, since the door handle fell off, but room 8 seemed no worse than expected, and I quickly did a washing (two pairs of pants and socks, and a tee shirt), then, tired as I was, I headed out to explore. I was now within striking distance of Timbuktu, and was starting to get excited, especially about my impending boat trip down the Niger.

First thing was to email home from a cybercafe. Since I wanted to roam a bit before it got too dark, I just dashed off a quick "I'm all right" message, and promised to do a long update the next day. It was already dark, and almost immediately I was surrounded by *guides*. These were something the same as the railway station touts, but mostly a bit younger, and they wanted to be my friend and show me round. Anything you want, they'll get. Nothing is too much trouble. They are your friends. They are pests.

One of them decided to really stick with me, and kept asking to be my guide while I was in Mopti. I knew that he only wanted a few pounds, but I really didn't want someone tagging along with me all the time. I knew I could find my way around a small place like Mopti perfectly well on my own. He was no real threat, but I decided to use a new tactic to lose him. I went back into the Cybercafe, and sat down. He hovered around the door for a while, and then since he obviously thought he might miss another opportunity with someone else, gave up on me, and left.

I nipped out and round a corner before he spotted me again, and for a wee while was able to wander around the dark streets on my own, drinking in the sights and sounds of a Mopti evening, but inevitably I was spotted, and had to shake off several more guides before I got to the *Bozo* restaurant on the other side of the harbour from my hotel. I had decided to head for the Bozo as I could see across the water that it was colourfully lit and would therefore probably be a tourist place with reasonable food. Ah.

It had been pretty difficult to navigate my way through the narrow harbour-side streets, and although I was no longer afraid in the dark, it was a struggle which I hoped would be well rewarded.

It turned out that the illuminations consisted of two coloured lanterns, which did indeed proclaim that this was a tourist destination, and to prove it, there was a party of 12 tourists, surrounded by about the same number of guides, just finishing a meal. Apart from my two kebabs at lunch time, I had eaten almost nothing all day, and was now ravenous, which was lucky, since my chicken was the scrawniest wee thing I've ever had the pleasure to eat, and the rice had obviously been boiled with the washing. The bread and beer were fine.

By the time I had finished, the tourist group had left in a mini-bus, and I had the place to myself, apart from the inevitable guide, but he didn't count, once I had impressed on him that *I didn't need a guide!*

It was lovely to sit there looking over the strange dark harbour, letting the breeze cool my skin, and even the coloured lanterns were somehow comforting. Since I had decided to stay in Mopti for two nights, I didn't feel the usual urgency to get to bed, so I was looking forward to a meander back to the hotel.

I got lost.

I only knew I was lost when people who seemed vaguely familiar to me started smiling, then laughing as I passed them for a third time. I could almost see my hotel across the harbour, but the route through the narrow winding streets and alleys eluded me. I wasn't panicked, but *was* lost. *If only I had a guide.*

Then, at last, in one dark street, I saw a taxi. There were four young lads hanging over it, and it was obviously getting a bit of TLC. Bits and pieces were lying on the street beside it, and one lad had his head under the bonnet. I knew I was taking a chance (Oh how much braver I was than when in Dakar), but decided to throw myself at their mercy, and asked if one of them could lead me to Le Campement Hotel. At first they looked at me as if I was mad, and then, after a quick huddled discussion amongst themselves, they were all smiles, and said certainly they would help. The tools were all gathered quickly up, and I was bundled into the taxi, along with the four lads. I had expected that perhaps one of them would simply lead me, walking back the three or four hundred yards to the hotel, but I now found myself white knuckled, hurtling through the dark and narrow streets of Mopti in a taxi full of young African guys, who thought the whole thing absolutely hilarious. The trip should have taken about three minutes. We arrived and screeched to a halt outside the hotel after ten minutes of "fun", and I was delighted to escape and give them 5,000 CFAs for their trouble. I could still hear them laughing as they sped away.

Steve, my Londoner friend from Bamako, was sitting on what passed for a patio, with a different African guide. All was in darkness. There was still no electricity. Had nobody paid the electricity bill? Probably not. It seemed that kind of place. I offered Steve a beer, and even though he had a large full glass in front of him, he gladly accepted. When I offered his companion a coke, he said no, but Steve said yes, for later. Perhaps Steve could be a drain on my finances. We sat in the dark, sipping our beers and chatting for a while and he told me that his previous guide; the one who had been with him in Bamako; had stolen his phone and disappeared. I hoped that his replacement guide would be a little more trustworthy, but looking at him, I doubted it. I decided to use a door wedge, which I had added to my pack at the last moment, for the first time that night. By nine o'clock, my cold was throbbing my head and churning my gut (or maybe it was the chicken yassa at the Bozo), so I disappointed Steve by saying that electricity or not, I was off to bed. Perhaps he was hoping for another free beer.

I slept well, and woke about 7.00 a.m. wondering what had happened to the call to prayer. Surely I hadn't slept through it! Could I be getting acclimatised? I was ravenous, but since there was still no electricity, there was no food at the inn. This gave me the moral excuse to head the mile or so up the riverside road to the Kanaga Hotel, where I had read that it was possible to buy a set price "all you can eat" breakfast. It had to be good. I wandered slowly, as if I was oh so used to doing this kind of thing, along beside the Niger, watching the early morning washers, and the boatmen preparing for the day. The low sun was colouring the far bank a pinky orange, and I was at ease with life. Even my cold seemed to be lifting.

The Kanaga lived up to its reputation. It was posh. Pilots stayed here, and all the well-heeled tourists. This was an oasis, and there was real appetising food. Granted, the breakfast was of the continental style. No bacon and eggs, but a 3,000 CFA buffet with coffee gave me all I could have hoped for. Once I felt full up enough to last a few hours, I asked at the reception desk if it would be possible to book a boat trip to Timbuktu. A rep for Bamara Tours, said he could probably get me onto a tourist pinasse for 14,000 CFAs, and we arranged to meet back at the hotel at 9.30 a.m. This gave me time to walk down the road a little to the Tourist Office, where two pleasant young men agreed that 14,000 CFAs was about right, and kindly stamped "Mopti" on my passport. They told me that it was expected in Mali that wherever you landed for the night you would get someone to stamp your passport so that your movements could be traced, and I was quite happy to comply, especially in Timbuktu, as a souvenir, but also since I definitely wanted to keep on the right side of the authorities.

Since I still had some time to kill, I sat and enjoyed the river scene, allowing the touts to pester me a little. At that time of day there weren't all that many of them, and those who did approach me were quite polite. I was intrigued to watch the varied array of "vehicles" used by the disabled touts, of which there were several, patrolling up and down the riverside. Most of these men seemed to have lost legs, or were paralysed in some way, but still managed to be mobile in "Heath Robinson" type tricycle contraptions, which all looked home-made. They could propel themselves along, pedalling by hand, fast enough to beat the able-bodied touts to any likely prospect who came along. Mostly they wanted to be a guide for the day, or simply begged for cash, but were cheery about it.

Back at the Kanaga, I met with the rep again, who now said that he could get me a place on a tourist pinasse for *140,000* CFAs, the equivalent of about £140! Since this was a ten-fold increase, I looked him in the eye, thanked him, and declined, so he then offered a place on a public pinasse for 40,000 CFAs. This annoyed me since the Tourist Office lads had told me that 20,000 CFAs would be the maximum for a public boat. Everyone wants a cut, but he wasn't getting it from me.

At the Tourist Office, they said "OK, ask for a boat owner called Guitey. He'll sort you out." At the harbour, no one had heard of him. I had probably written it down wrong. The day was becoming frustrating, and I was starting to worry that I might not get a boat at all! Eventually, with lots of help, I managed to buy a ticket for 20,000 CFAs on what they called the *Petit Baba* which appeared to be a two hundred foot long black-painted dug-out canoe with an upper covered deck over its length. It was made of steel though, and was one of the more civilised looking craft on the river. My ticket entitled me to the trip (one way), a place to sleep (a section of the metal floor on the *lux* upper deck), and food en route. I was advised to get a rattan mat to lie on, since otherwise I would end up filthy from the floor. Kate had already suggested that it would be worthwhile to get a foam mattress to sleep on, for warmth and comfort. The young guide who was currently advising and helping me, of course, could sell me a rattan mat – for 2,500 CFAs, but I said I would look around, since I was sure I had seen them for 1,000. So I literally had *a ticket to Timbuktu* for the following day. Things were looking up.

First, I spent an hour and a half on the internet, with Kate. She was concerned about my health, and insisted that I get a *good* foam mattress and a blanket for the boat trip. We arranged that she would attempt to phone me at the Kanaga at 8.00 p.m. that evening, if possible. Then, before I could start looking for the mattress (there were lots of shops selling them), I bumped into the two rude best-seat-taking women from my previous bus trip. In chatting, I discovered that they were Flemish and were staying at a Catholic Mission where they had brought money, donated by others. This gave them free accommodation. My opinion of them didn't change, and then they off-loaded their guide on to me, and waved goodbye.

I decided to make use of this new companion, and he helped me to buy a one inch thick foam mattress, with a very striking multi-coloured cloth cover, which I was able to roll up small enough to carry under my arm. For some strange reason, this really lifted my spirits, and made me feel that perhaps I was actually becoming a *real Traveller*.

By now it was well past lunch time, so I headed to the Bozo again, this time noting the return route! Chips and beer with a view over the harbour passed a very pleasant hour. The harbour was really just a mud-bottomed, large man-made inlet from the Bani River, which opened into the Niger. Drawn up all round the edge of the shallow sloped stone-paved banks, were dozens of pinasses; long, wide canoe shaped wooden boats; mostly black with brightly painted bows. They looked about thirty to forty feet long, and had roofs over their length, consisting of hooped wooden bearers, covered in canvas. This would be a necessity on long river journeys in the sun. There was constant movement, with boats, laden with people and goods, coming and going to a backdrop of barter and trade along the banks. The sight was more fulfilling than the food.

Again I dawdled on the way back, not because I was lost this time, but because I was fascinated by the sights and sounds around me. These were sights and sounds that I don't usually experience in Inverness (well not often). Goats tied up in plastic bags, on top of a mini-bus, (turn a goat on its back; tie all four feet together; place the goat in a large plastic bag, with only its head sticking out; tie the bag round its neck; fling your *parcel* up on to the roof-rack; job done), Tuaregs in turbans and flowing robes on mopeds, stalls of what at first sight appeared to be slabs of ice, but were actually salt (brought across the Sahara in camel trains) and men making nails by hand.

I stood and watched the nail makers for a long time. There was a line of about ten men squatting on the ground under a very dilapidated tarpaulin cover, each with his own tiny furnace, powered by air from a bicycle-wheel driven pump, operated by a young assistant. This was indeed a sweat shop, but everyone seemed quite happy and there was plenty good-natured banter, none of which I could understand, but I guessed that some was directed at me, a gawking tourist. This was a small part of a boat building yard where the long wooden pinasses were produced, and I could have watched all day. I ended up buying five of the long nails that one man had just made in front of me.

Later, at Le Campement, I again met Steve who was sitting with a young Australian couple. They told me that they were heading to Timbuktu that night on the last trip of the season for the main public passenger boat. They had booked an *en-suite cabin*, and would have a double bed! No one had told me about this! I could have gone in style. I had missed my chance. Then they told me the price. 50,000 CFAs each!

I settled back with my beer, and wished them a good trip.

I was now becoming excited at the prospect of talking to Kate on the phone, so on the way to the Kanaga, I emailed her to say that I would be there at about 8 p.m. and if she just phoned and asked for "Joe", I would be hovering near the reception desk.

It worked! At 8 o'clock on the dot, I was sitting in the lounge, in a chair near reception, trying to look as if I had every right to be there, when I heard the phone ring on the desk. I couldn't tell that it was Kate, so had to wait and watch, as the old receptionist started to say "Joe? Joe?" When I saw him starting to look at the reception computer, I knew I wouldn't be on it, so quickly bounced up to the desk, and said "I'm Joe". He gave me a very puzzled look, and handed me the phone.

Oh, I wanted to pour everything out, the journey so far, the plans, my love, but nothing is ever perfect. There was so much noise at reception that I could hardly hear her, and almost immediately, I started getting disapproving looks from the receptionist, so it was a short, but very sweet conversation, and I walked back to my hotel in the dark, with a spring in my step, un-fazed by the tall very dark people, dressed in flowing rags who approached me with a menacing air and a quiet "Ca va?"

The evening ended with two beers with Steve, who appeared to be more and more detached from reality, and I wondered, as I said goodnight and goodbye, whether he would survive for much longer in Africa.

The next morning, Friday the 19th, was the day I would at last sail down the Niger to Timbuktu. The journey would be about 300 kilometres, and I had no idea how long it would take. An adventure!

Since I was told that the boat would be leaving about mid-day, I had time to return to the Kanaga for breakfast. It was again, of course, a beautiful morning and returning to Le Campement, I enjoyed the sight of a young girl winnowing grain by throwing it up into the air and catching the good bits, as the morning breeze blew away the chaff, while near her on the river bank, sat some men making winnowing sieves. Then there were the butchers' stalls, with heads and feet of animals spread around them, on the ground. Some sights are uplifting, others not so. Coming towards me through the small crowd at the stalls was something I hadn't seen before. A young boy carrying a wooden slatted framework over which were draped several folds of blue, black, and brown cloth. These were the makings of the Tuareg turbans which were much in evidence in Mopti. I couldn't stop myself, and although the cloth is relatively heavy, and I had a long way to go, I bought some of the blue. However, not out of mean-ness, but for practicality, I only bought 2 metres - half the length that the young lad suggested would make me "A real Tuareg."

Although my ticket included food, the boat journey could be a couple of days long, so I decided it would be a good idea to take some *emergency rations,* other than just the two delicious croissants I had stolen from the Kanaga breakfast bar. First thing was a yellow and green striped plastic bucket, obviously from the same factory as the plastic kettles, and into this went bananas, a tin of sardines (*what was I thinking of?*), crisps, bread, some other tasty bites, and three large bottles of water.

As with most of the places I had so far stayed in, Le Campement didn't seem so bad, now that I was leaving it.

Looking round over a last beer, I started to think that the tables were really quite nicely done, with cloths and flowers, but housed in what appeared to be an air-raid shelter which had suffered a near miss. *I* wouldn't miss this place though. I took a Diacalm (for the journey), and nodded a goodbye to the owner.

Now for the boat. Having no idea when it would actually leave, I was anxious to get on, in case I missed it. That would be disaster, but I had to try a little email to Kate first, before I went. I just had to say "*I'm off to Timbuktu!*"

7. PASSAGE TO TIMBUKTU

It was about noon when I climbed on board, and found myself a spot on the floor of the upper deck, with my back to a side bench, and plenty of space to spread out my nice new foam mat, which was almost double bed size. Looking across the deck which was about 5 metres wide, I had a good view of the river bank through one of the big square holes which served as windows. There was plenty space because I appeared to be the only person there! This was a bit worrying. Was I on the right boat? Was there something I didn't know? I had started the day feeling intrepid, but now trepidation started to creep up on me again.

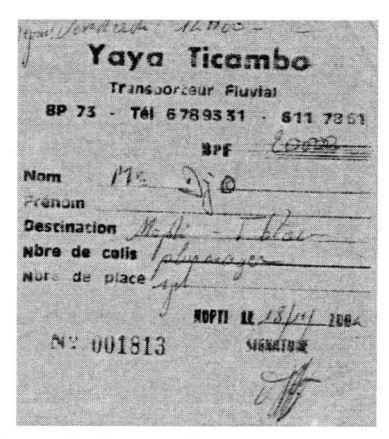

Then the hassling started. First, I was happy enough for the company, and allowed myself to be convinced that it was a rule that every passenger must have a rattan mat, even if they have a foam mattress. This was to ensure that the metal floor would not be damaged. Oh yes. Anyway, I gave a youngster 1,000 CFAs and surprisingly he returned with a mat for me, which appeared new. It was easier to refuse the trinket sellers, and when an old guy came on and told me that I needed to buy a permit to go to Timbuktu, I realised that I had become a *mark,* and was a bit rude.

Time was going on, and I became increasingly anxious. Surely I wasn't going to be the only passenger. Luckily the activity on the shore was diverting, with people bringing a huge variety of goods, from blankets to melons, and stacking them alongside. Bizarrely I could also see a flying saucer! It looked like it had just landed in the town beyond the top of the river bank, and no-one had noticed! Looking with my *sensible* eyes on, I decided it was actually a large concrete saucer shaped water tower, and was not Martian. So often, ancient and modern were encompassed by the same view. There was a "Bittar-Trans" stall where it appeared that tickets for the boat were being sold, but still no one came on to join me, except for those who wanted to sell something.

Thankfully a young man and his toddler son and a rucksack eventually arrived and sat down on the side bench near me. At last, a fellow passenger. I attempted a bit of conversation with him, but it was very difficult. When I asked him when the boat would be leaving he said "Soon", which was encouraging, but I really didn't fancy a day and a half on a boat with such little company.

Travelling solo has one major drawback. There is no one to watch your stuff. So if you want to go somewhere, all your stuff goes with you, or it might not be there when you get back. This meant that although I now fancied buying one of the huge water melons which were being sold on the shore, I would have had to take my gear with me off the boat to get one, or leave it there, which I wasn't sure would be wise. Eventually the young man solved my problem. He offered to go and get me a melon, and said it should only be about 500 CFAs, but returned quite soon to tell me that the cheapest he could get was 1,500! I was becoming too long in the tooth to fall for that, so told him to forget it, and he then produced one for 700 CFAs. I was getting the hang of this, but being kind, gave him 1,000. He, and his child then got off the boat, and I never saw them again! He had simply been another chancer, but I admired his style.

Since I was yet again the only person on board, at least on the *lux* deck, I decided I could take a little look around. The front of the boat at that level was loaded with stacks of brightly covered foam mattresses like mine, but much thicker. This seemed to be cargo, but there were also lots of travel bags, many of them piled on the roof of the lux above me. In the middle of the boat, between the lux and the mattresses was an open space with a large iron *witches' cauldron* type cooking pot at one side. All this was on the upper level, and I didn't venture to look downstairs at the lower reaches of the boat. I preferred to be where I could see my gear, and when a policeman appeared on the gangplank, I quickly went back to my place. The first thing the cop did was come over to me, and ask if he could share my rattan mat! I am as generous as the next man, but this seemed a bit forward. However, this was *authority* and I wasn't going to argue.

"Yes, of course."

He then started eyeing up my foam mattress! No way! I changed the situation by getting up and walking to the window, hoping that he wouldn't requisition my bed behind my back. Now, more real passengers started to come on. They were a very varied assortment. There were girls with what looked like brown tattooed dots round their mouths, and a couple of young lads, one with a guitar who spoke reasonable English. Unfortunately I had discovered that I was losing my voice! The cold was obviously still with me, and I was starting to feel a chill from the breeze blowing through the deck. God, what if I lost my voice completely! I decided to speak as little as possible for a while.

Soon the boat was filling up, and when a large lady with a screed of kids plunked herself down on the spare half of my rattan mat while the cop was away, I bolted back and lay out full length on *my* half to book it. The kids had huge sticking out belly buttons, but were otherwise very normal and loud. Next, a couple of really beautiful young girls with very fancy beaded head-dresses took a spot opposite me. I noticed that their feet and hands were tattooed with the same patterns as the other girls' mouths, and they were wearing nail varnish. Then came a big family, the mother in brown and white robes, carrying a potty which appeared to be too big to be of any use to her kids. My once empty lux was now becoming busy and I wondered just how crowded it might get. Not as bad as the Alham, surely. A woman to my right started eating a fish by tearing it apart with her hands. Head, tail and bits were hurled over the side. With the delicate state of my stomach, this was not what I wanted to watch, especially when the flies started to congregate. Oh Lord, what kind of journey was *this* going to be? Luckily the cop returned and caused a diversion by unceremoniously ejecting the woman who was on his side of *my* mat.

One of the young lads started to chat, and although my voice was a croak, it was good to have a bit of conversation. He explained that *the head-dress girls* were artisans who made the head-dresses in their village somewhere down river and had probably been in Mopti to sell them. Their tattoos were in fact only henna, which they probably had had applied in town, and would wear off within a couple of weeks. The next, and much more interesting bit of information, was that the cop was not a policeman, but a conservation worker in a green uniform! I had given up half my bed to a park ranger! I looked at him, and he immediately told me that he would prefer if I moved my mat to a different position which suited him better. *He was not a cop*! I said no.

It was now 5.30 p.m. I had been on the boat for five and a half hours and was still in Mopti. Or was this Timbuktu? Had I slept through the whole journey? Was I hallucinating again? No, I was still there, so I asked the erstwhile cop, if he knew when we would be leaving.

"After evening prayers."
Ah.

I started to feel a vibration. Could it be the engine starting, or was I getting the shivers? It was the shivers. Obviously I was going to be cold overnight.

Boredom was starting to grip me. There were only so many interesting characters that I could take in in a day, and I had had my fill. Then I started to fart. This was a cause for concern for everyone, so I quickly delved into the top of my rucksack, and downed a couple more Diacalms. My hope was that I would have no need of the *facilities* on board, whatever they were. I guessed they would be rudimentary.

To relieve the boredom I counted the passengers in the lux, and found that there were 19 adults and 7 kids, which still left a bit of space. I had just decided to count them again when we were off! Just like that. No one cheered, in fact I seemed to be the only one who noticed, or was bothered. Then again, I had been waiting for this moment for six hours and ten minutes. Or perhaps I had been waiting for this for the whole of my life.

It was now dark, as we ghosted along past some faintly silhouetted islands with a few dim lights. Occasionally we slipped past a long fishing pirogue. It all seemed other-worldly. There was no engine noise and little to indicate that we were moving at all; as if we were drifting in space.

By 8 o'clock many of my fellow passengers were asleep, mostly without even the protection of a rattan mat as they lay on the steel floor. I assumed that this was what they were used to. Most had taken their shoes off when they arrived, probably because it would be bad form to stand on a neighbour's things (or head) with your shoes on. I took off my shoes.

Those not asleep were chatting quietly, and even the kids were quiet. It would not have been the same on a ferry on the Clyde. I toyed with the idea of going to find the galley which I assumed would be the witches' cauldron I had seen earlier, but thought better of it. Food could wait for a while yet.

As I drifted off to sleep on my double-thickness foam mattress, (I had folded it in two to thwart the erstwhile cop) all snuggled in my sleeping bag, with my Tuareg cloth round my neck, I wondered how the captain could see other boats in the dark. I doubted that the boat had radar. By 9.00 p.m. I was asleep.

I slept amazingly well – until 5.00 a.m. when we stopped at a village to load on some goods. At that time in the morning it was still dark, and the activity on the river bank was carried out quietly so as not to disturb the rest of the village. As with so many things I had seen on the trip, this was way outside my normal life, and I was revelling in the situation. An hour or so later, as I drank some steaming coffee and ate a little bread at the galley, I watched as two sleek felucca type sailing boats were driven past us by a cool morning breeze in the thin pre-dawn light.

Since all was quiet on board, I decided it was time to investigate the toilet arrangements. These were located down below in the lower deck, where I discovered that a fire was already lit under their cauldron. I had never seen an open fire being burned on the deck of a boat before, but assumed it was ok, since the floor was steel, and there was plenty of water around if all went wrong. The toilet was a hole in the back of the boat. Just a hole. There was no seat, no nothing, except a door for privacy. I did try to make use of these facilities, but since I could actually see through the door which was a thin bit of hessian sack, I found it just too public, and gave up. There was no way that I was going to squat there with the hundred or so folk in these nether regions watching *my* nether regions. Their lot was certainly not as "lux" as ours, but I still wasn't going to alleviate it by being entertainment. I retreated to my patch, and took another couple of Diacalms.

Most folk were now awake, and carrying out their morning activities, which consisted of sitting looking into space. I decided to brighten things up by taking photos, which I promised to send to various people when I got home. Agaly, my English speaking young student friend told me to send the one of the *head-dress girls* to the captain of the boat, since very few people have an actual postal address, and in fact there was no real post as we know it. His photo was to go to a hotel in Bamako, and the "cop" actually had an address. It's not particularly simple to pass a whole day just sitting on a boat in the middle of a wide calm river, with only the flat sand banks on the horizon to look at, so any diversion is welcomed. While I was sitting up on top, a tourist pinasse came by, and all the clean, white holidaymakers jumped up and took photos of our *authentic* river boat crammed with a couple of hundred black faces looking back at them – and one solitary white face with a camera taking *their* photo in return. Small things, but it passed the day.

Since there were only a few kids in the lux I decided that I had enough little lollipops to offer round to them. Feeding frenzy! The kids had to fight the adults for a lollipop! This was no good, so in a very stern voice I declared that these were for children only *"Seulement les enfants!"* It worked, but I did notice a couple of the kids crying after their mum had taken them off to the side.

Agaly seemed to be grooming me. He was certainly very helpful and friendly, but was starting to feed some "hard-luck" stories into the conversation. I also noticed that when his friend with the guitar started to speak to me, there was a rapid exchange of unintelligible words, and the friend went back to his own corner. Could Agaly have said "Leave him. This one's mine." I wondered, however with the prospect of spending hours just watching kids with runny noses (mine was too) and people just sitting, I was happy to have Agaly's friendship, false or not.

I decided to teach him "The Address to the Haggis".

Well, I had a haggis, or at least the melon could double as one, so I explained a little about Robert Burns, and Burns Night, and then launched into it. As I said, anything for a diversion.

When I came to "His knife, see rustic labour dicht and cut ye up wi' ready slicht," I took out my unused flick knife, pressed the catch producing its sparkly long blade with a satisfying click, and disembowelled the melon.

It wasn't the poetry, or even the knife (they probably all had one) that got a reaction, it was the prospect of another food hand out, and this time the adults were going to get their share! I could see they were all anxious, especially the *cop,* so did an abridged version of the Address, cut out a small piece for myself then handed the rest plus the knife to Agaly to distribute. Once he had dealt with the scrum that developed, and all was peaceful again, I wrote down the first two verses for him, and he very quickly learned them, complete with *my* accent.

He is probably now making lots of extra cash in Bamako bars. All this put poetry, an old friend of mine, into my mind, and I penned a little one of my own, sitting alone among these strange people.

I'll go to Timbuktu without you.
I can do that so easily.
I'm an independent man
And can find my way to distant places
Take plenty paces, big and small,
That's all I need to do,
Without you,
To prove myself to me.

But I have cried for you in Africa,
And yearned for you to touch.
So much I love you that it hurts.
And now I know I cannot be alone.
You have been with me every minute of this trip
And I understand and thank a god
That he has joined us at the hip.

Perhaps it wasn't my best ever poem, but at that moment it struck the right chord.

For another diversion, I decided to chance eating something from the "*WRVS* stall" up top. The menu was rice with bits (probably meat). It was delicious, but I decided that one helping would be enough. Not wishing to tempt fate, or my stomach, I took two more Diacalm.

By mid-afternoon, my repertoire of diversions was getting pretty depleted, and I was wishing that someone else would do something. But no. So I taught the head-dress girls, who spoke Songai and nothing else, how to say "My name is … What is your name?" and Agaly helped me to write down their names phonetically. He said that that would be the first time they had ever seen their names written, so I tore the page out of my notebook and gave it to them. They were delighted, but I regretted not keeping a copy for myself.

Next it was noughts and crosses with the kids (and adults), and lastly, I taught a little boy how to make a paper aeroplane. We flew it all over the cabin, then out into the big grey river. Children are fun, no matter where you are.

All that remained was to have the cop dress me up, winding his long piece of black cloth round my head and face as a Tuareg turban. We tried my cloth, but as the little seller boy had predicted, it was far too short, and kept falling off, much to the mirth of my fellow passengers.

Now exhausted, I retreated to the forward end of the cargo deck and lay on a mattress destined for someone's bed in the desert, goodness knows where.

I hid for a while.

One of the small luxuries I had allowed myself was a bottle of very concentrated orange which, when mixed with water, served to take away the taste of unusual food and unusual living. Every time I took a swig, Agaly would ply me with questions about it, obviously wanting some. Eventually I told him loudly that it was medicine for my sore stomach. This did not do the trick. He said that he too had a sore stomach.

I then lied a little more. I informed him, and everyone else, who was listening, that my sore stomach came from a major operation I had had and that if I didn't keep drinking this stuff I would die. I then put on a *face* and took a couple of swigs. They all murmured in sympathy, and I nodded my thanks. OK, so it was my only luxury.

Later in the afternoon, lots of people got off at a village, including the head-dress girls and most of the kids. I was sorry to see them go. They had added colour and a bit of fun to the trip. As they left, I took some photographs of the girls standing with perfect balance in the middle of one of the many long thin pinasses which came out from the shore to pick up the passengers. I noticed that these boats all had some firewood strewn along the floor, making standing in them even more of a feat. When I looked more closely, I saw that some larger boats were full of broken branches and twigs, and it dawned on me that everywhere I looked there were people on the shore, holding buckets full of wood, or even carrying baskets of wood on their heads. Firewood, it appeared, was not just a commodity, but almost a currency in the desert. I assumed that most of it would be flotsam collected from the river to sell to the surrounding villages.

Contrary to most of my expectations, the people leaving the boat, heading to a "poor" life in a mud-hut village on the banks of the Niger, seemed perfectly happy and content with their lot. They waved me a farewell, and smiled.

The night was very disturbed. It was like trying to sleep in a noisy, moving travellers' encampment, with the boat stopping often at various villages to allow people and goods to come on and get off. I slept fitfully, but at some time in the night, woke to find a lull in the activity. All was quiet.

Sitting in the black darkness of the boat, humming through the still waters of the Niger night, I was alone. All around me, the black bodies lay, some contorted into grotesque shapes that would have terrified me, had I not already become familiar with them.

I lay back on the thin foam mat, clasped my hands behind my head on my rucksack pillow and pondered how I came to be in this strange, exciting place.

It was difficult to settle my mind, to steady the whirling memories of places, incidents and people that crowded in, clamouring for my attention - Michael, my temporary French travelling companion being so nearly gored by the badly tethered bad-tempered cow at the taxi-rank; the utterly confusing border crossing that I could not have negotiated without his French; the incident with the teen-age louts and the robed Chief of Police in Kayes; or the hot tears I wept on the bus, to the embarrassment of the leathery old Tuareg beside me.

The memories, ah the memories, gathered in two short, packed weeks.

Even the last twelve hours filled me with sensation.

I played through my mind, images of my fellow passengers; the burly, green uniformed *cop* who demanded a share of my rattan mat; the large serious, suspicious Mama with her many children hidden among the folds of her multi-coloured skirts; Agaly, the young, English speaking student, who befriended me, and warned his friend not to get involved; and the head-dress girls - beautiful, young, and so gaily adorned with their beads, who saw themselves written, for the first time in their lives, when this strange white man took out his pen and asked their names. And the others- dark, strange, forbidding.

And there was no other white face but mine.

Now I lay on the floor, alone, with the cop who wasn't a cop, to my right, and the friend who maybe wasn't a friend to my left, and the wizened old goat-herd with the all too real curved dagger through his belt, at my feet. A moment of panic as I understood just how alone, and how vulnerable I was in this oh-so-foreign place, and then, a warm feeling filled my whole being, as I realised that after almost 50 years of yearning, I was at last living my own Enid Blyton adventure. Then I slept.

The morning was beautiful, and I took in the sunrise with coffee and bread at the galley up top. I was feeling good despite the ever lingering cold, and was able to gently put off the woman who almost demanded that I give her my plastic bucket, since I "had no need for it." She was right, but I decided that *I* would decide who got the bucket.

Word was that we would arrive at Korioumé, the port for Timbuktu, at about 10.00 a.m. so it was a pleasant surprise to find us suddenly there at quarter to nine!

Timbuktu is about 18 kilometres to the North of the river, and each boat is met by a phalanx of Landrovers and 4x4s. My guide book told me that the fare should be about 500 CFAs, but I might have to haggle, however Agaly, who had "won" the plastic bucket for his help, said that I was not to worry because he could arrange things for me. I stood on the sloping shore, saying my farewells to the *cop* and others, and watched Agaly approach the driver at the furthest end of the line of transport. When he returned, he was smiling, and told me it was all fixed and would only cost me 10,000 CFAs! My heart sank, as I realised that my plastic bucket had been misplaced.

"No" I simply said, and watched Agaly's face as he realised that he had over-done it. Splitting the fare with the driver, he would have stood to make about 5,000 CFAs, plus a bucket, out of me. I wasn't pleased and told him what my book suggested the fare should be. He didn't offer to re-negotiate, and when I said that I would find a different driver, both he and his pal assured me that if I tried, no-one would take me on.

"We'll see." I thought, and headed for Agaly's driver.

"How much to Timbuktu, please?" I said nicely, making it obvious that my book was open at the appropriate page.

"Ten thousand."

"I don't want to buy your Landrover, I only want a lift to Timbuktu."

This was intended to raise a smile, but perhaps it didn't translate into French as a joke so well, or maybe I was just too tired to realise that it wasn't funny. His attitude became a little brittle and he told me I could do as I pleased.

"OK, I'll walk!" and I headed back along to pick up my pack.

"All right, 2,000, and you can sit at the front."

I climbed in to the preferred front seat, as Agaly squeezed in the back. I was soon joined by a distinguished looking man, wearing pristine white robes. He was obviously *special* too, and I imagined that he must have been on the Hadj to Mecca, but he did not respond to my attempts to speak to him. Considering that I hadn't washed, shaved or changed my clothes for two days, and had slept in them on the floor of a dusty boat, I imagine he just wanted to keep a space between himself and me. Where he had come from, I couldn't tell, since I hadn't seen him on the boat. Another surprise was seeing a white face in the back of the Land Rover. I certainly hadn't noticed another white on the boat, but perhaps he had been on the lower, less lux deck.

Just before we set off, the driver demanded my 2,000 CFAs, and *"500 for your friend!"* I gave him 3,000, and even let Agaly keep the bucket. He got off before Timbuktu, and as he left, I suggested we meet up for a drink the next day. He declined my offer. He was Muslim.

The road between Korioumé and Timbuktu is good tarmac, and it wasn't long before I gave a little silent cheer as we passed through the big mud-brick "South Gate", emblazoned with "Ville de Tombouctou" in tiles on the arch above it.

I had arrived!

PHOTOS

Tambacounda Gare Routier.

The Alham from Dibola to Kayes.

Making nails in Mopti.

Mopti harbour

The Petit Baba.

The head-dress girls.

A posh tourist pinasse.

Up top at the galley.

Mopti Mosque

Al Haat Patisserie, Timbuktu.

Timbuktu street.

Typical compound near the Sahara Passion.

Early morning whisky for monkey and me with Flamme de la Paix Monument in background.

Outside Mac's Refuge

Pounding the maize

Yoff beach.

8. TIMBUKTU

We were all dumped off in the street near the *Petit Marché,* and as the locals disappeared, I was left with the other white guy. Before we could even begin to talk, we were pounced on by two local guides, with offers of everything we might desire, but especially accommodation.

Since I was pretty disorientated, and my companion quite reticent, I decided that this was a good time to actually *accept* the offer of a guide, and told them I wanted to go to the Sahara Passion hotel, which according to my book was "basic, but good value." The map in the book was also basic, so the guides were invaluable. My new companion said he would accompany me, and as we were led via a very tortuous route through many narrow alleys, (no doubt to justify their tip) he told me that he was French, and had joined the boat early that morning, having been staying with friends in one of the riverside villages. He was young, but obviously a seasoned lone traveller, and gave his name as Jacques, without venturing a surname. He said he would sleep in the Sahara Passion that night, and then stay with friends in the town. I was impressed to think that he had so many friends this far into Africa, but remembered that I had read that in Timbuktu it is not allowed for private houses to do "B&B", however, if you are just staying with *"friends"– that's all right then.* Jacques obviously knew the score, and would be making some enquiries in the morning. I would never have had the nerve to attempt that. It might be much cheaper, but I just didn't have the language. Anyway, I fancied some luxury.

Jacques, on the other hand, with his tanned thin face, dusty old rucksack, and well-worn clothes looked as if he had been in the wilds for quite a while and was relishing it. Actually, he looked like something from "Carry on up the Khyber".

I wondered if I would end up looking like that by the time I got home. Wow, *me*.

After about ten minutes' walking, the guides brought us to a street corner at the north-west edge of town where we were confronted by a small green door in a high wall. There was nothing to tell us that this was the hotel, or in fact, any hotel, but they simply pressed the bell in the wall and held out their hands. I paid each of them 1,000 CFAs, but Jacques ignored them. Ah.

The door was opened by a fairly small, pleasant-faced African in a long blue robe, over tee-shirt and jeans. He was wearing pink flip flops, and had a most engaging smile.

This was Belli, the caretaker. The guides left and he invited us in.

The Sahara Passion was all that I had expected. It was a simple, single storey mud-brick building set in a compound with a dusty sandy yard, and a couple of outbuildings. There was a plain veranda with a table and chairs, which appeared to be the office/ breakfast bar, all shaded by a few trees round the edge. Here and there some shrubs lent a little interest, with their pretty pink and white flowers. Apart from the flora, everything was the same colour – sand. To me it looked like heaven. I was going to rest here for a few days. Rest at last.

As we were led inside, I noticed that there was a stairway up to the roof and could hardly wait to get my first real view of Timbuktu.

Belli offered the last available room to Jacques, who refused it and said he would like to sleep on the floor of the common room, if that was ok. He was obviously on a *very* tight budget. So I got the room. I hadn't expected luxury, and didn't get it, but twin beds, made from intertwined thin tree branches topped with multi-coloured foam mattress, mosquito nets and a fan was all that I could have asked at that point. Except – there was no shower or toilet, and I expected to really need a toilet soon. The Diacalm were wearing off. Oh well, we can't always have everything we want in life and I had spotted "facilities" just down the hall as we came in.

What the hell, *I WAS IN TIMBUKTU*!

And, I had slept in worse in Scotland.

The hotel had, of course, no bar and no restaurant, but just across the road, according to my book was the Amanar Restaurant which was highly recommended.

Since I was, I knew, looking a mess, the priority was to get spruced up a bit. Having a shower, although in cold water, was bliss and doing my laundry at the same time was sensible. This consisted of throwing all my dirty clothes (*all* my clothes) on the floor, and trampling them as I showered. The shower itself was a *wet room* in the corner of the building, and was dank, but I wasn't going to spend my life there. Next, I needed a shave. Two days' stubble was making me feel unkempt and I was looking forward to that delicious fresh feel after a good, slow, careful close shave.

My razor was broken! It had only been a simple semi-disposable plastic thing, and had served me well, but I must have sat on it on the boat and decapitated it. Hey ho, shaving could wait.

It was difficult to decide what to do first. I wanted to look from the roof. I wanted to see the dunes of the Sahara. I wanted to explore Timbuktu. I wanted to e-mail Kate to say I had made it. I wanted to eat. I needed to dry some clothes, so hung the necessities out of the bedroom window for half an hour while I fought off sleep. Eventually, hunger won, so I put on a damp tee shirt and trousers, pocketed my little wind-up monkey pal and headed across the street to the Amanar where I was pleasantly surprised. It was like a little Greek taverna complete with flies, but with a splendid view of the Sahara and a magnificent big monument, only a few metres away. There was very little but sand between its front gate and North Africa.

Spag Boll and a bottle of Flag went down very well, while Tamimou, a young man from Togo, made me welcome.

As I was anxious to contact *control,* I asked a waiter where the nearest internet café was.

"There is only one, to the south of the town, about half an hour's walk, but don't go today. This is Sunday. It will be shut."

Shut on a Sunday! I thought Mali was a *Muslim* country. Damn!

However, Tamimou had overheard, and came to my table to assure me that the internet café *would* be open. That was better, and I thought it would be wise to go and find it, open or not. I wanted to walk through Timbuktu anyway.

For many, Timbuktu is a disappointment. They come, expecting to find something extraordinary. After all, the name is almost legendary, as a far-away, impossible-to-reach gold-paved paradise. But in reality, Timbuktu is just a small African market town, on the southern edge of the Sahara Desert, with, on the surface, not a lot to entice the visitor except its name. Most of the town is built in a grid pattern with the buildings mainly mud brick, the houses being single storey, many in compounds, and the commercial buildings a storey higher. Everything is the colour of the sand underfoot. Along the streets some scrubby trees give a little shade, next to doorways, and garbage is everywhere. In an area where there is precious little rainfall, even a paper bag takes a while to disintegrate. Plastic is forever, and I couldn't help but be aware of the accumulated rubbish in most corners. The middle of the town is the old part, with narrow winding intimate alleyways, markets, and mosques. In a big open area near the Petit Marché there was what appeared to be a river of trash coming out from a side street, and disappearing into the sand in the middle of the square. To my eye, it was all quite unsavoury, and unhygienic. To the eyes of the residents, it is probably invisible.

It did seem that Sunday was a day of rest, since although there was plenty of evidence of stalls, many of them at house doors, there was very little commerce going on. I meandered through the wide streets and little alleys till I came to Independence Square at the south end of the town. Here, the buildings changed, and became more imposing.

The Marie, or Town Hall, sat to one side, with other important looking buildings dotted round the edge. In the middle was a rather rough and arid garden. Although mud bricks were still very much in evidence, concrete was starting to show itself. I would have been tempted to take a photo or two, but on one side of the square was the entrance to an army camp, with two guards on duty, and I just knew that it wouldn't be a wise move.

The long, straight road, south of here, the one I had arrived on, was the only tarmac in Timbuktu, and either led out, or in, depending on one's perspective, or mood.

This area was where a lot of the government buildings were to be found, along with NGO offices etc. and had a slightly more prosperous air than the older parts. It was also where the Post Office was (it was shut), and across the road from there was the internet café.

At first sight, I didn't hold out much hope of contacting base from there. It was a small concrete shed-like building which certainly *appeared* to be closed. My heart sank. It had taken me almost an hour to reach it from the hotel, and this, I had been told, was the *only* internet café in town. I tried the door. It opened. Inside was a bare room with a few computer set-ups, and two of the most laid-back helpers I had ever come across. The speed of the internet connection almost perfectly matched the speed of these two lads. Slow (and not very reliable).

It may have been that this internet café was intended really for local use only, since very few of the tourists who visit Timbuktu stayed long enough to find it, far less use it. They possibly had connections in their hotels anyway. I didn't.

Luckily, I *did* have time, and persevered until I had sent the message to Kate –

I MADE IT! -
No, that's not true. WE MADE IT –
You, me, and monkey, are in TIMBUKTU!

I then gave her the full story of the boat trip, and arrival, and suggested that we should both try to synchronise our emailing the next day at 12 noon, for a chat. I hoped that it would work, but had big doubts since the connection was so poor.

Outside again, it was time to head north to see the dunes at last, but when I reached what I reckoned to be the very middle of the town, near the Grand Marché I stopped, and did something much more important. Standing in the middle of this little African town, I turned my face up to the sky, to Heaven, laughed, and whispered,

"*Hey Mum, look, I'm in Timbuktu!*"

I'm sure I heard her reply –

"Och you, away ......"

Wandering north again, I bumped into the Australian couple, Damien and Joanna, whom I had first met in Mopti. We had a drink and a chat in the Al Hayat Patisserie and they told me that they were lucky to have made it to Timbuktu. Their posh river ferry (with the en-suite cabin) had been scraping the bed of the river, and it had been literally touch and go.

They did make it however, and were in the Boctou Hotel, which was a few notches up from the Sahara Passion. They were quite excited, as they were due to meet up with a guide, who would show them a camel train, about to leave for the North across the desert. I wished them luck, and they promised to tell me about it later.

Now, at last, I was going to walk in the desert. I patted my pocket to make sure that my monkey was still in one piece, and headed north. On the way, I bought a "Gillette Style" razor in a dark little house/shop, and dropped it off at my room. It seemed a bit expensive to me at 450 CFAs, but I was desperate, and really looking forward to that nice hot shave.

The Sahara comes to the door of the Sahara Passion, and flows beyond it into the town. It threatens to swallow up Timbuktu, but somehow has been defeated over many, many years. Now I only had to walk a few hundred yards north, past the huge memorial arch of the Flamme de la Paix to feel that I was right in the desert. As I skliffed my feet along a little valley between two gigantic dunes, I was amazed to meet my Aussie friends heading in the opposite direction. They looked a little unhappy, and said that unfortunately the camel train had left before they had got to it. For some reason I didn't feel surprised. Now, two Tuaregs, in full costume were taking them to their tent for tea. The younger Tuareg asked if I would like to join them. I could just tell that this was a commercial venture, not a magnanimous offer, so thanked him, and said that as I was about to collect some sand, I wouldn't have time to join them.

"OK, after sand, you come to tent."

"I'm sorry, no, I'm going to write to my wife after I get the sand."

I managed to pass them and got a few steps away, before the young guy came after me and had one last try.

"You want necklaces for your wife? I have good necklaces."

"Not today thanks." and I fled, leaving the Aussies to their fate.

It did cross my mind that he hadn't blinked when I told him it would take time to collect sand. I was standing on sand. Actually I was quite excited about collecting my first Sahara sand, and I wanted it to be from the top of a real dune. Everyone needs a hobby.

I didn't go very far from the town, since the prospect of finding my way back across the dunes in the dark was a bit daunting for my first night, but scrambling up a particularly high dune, gave me a wonderful viewpoint. About half a mile to the south was the monument and then the town, with its big mosque, and a water tower just visible in the distance. Around me were scattered Tuareg tents, which looked like they were being lived in on a permanent basis. I had read that this was so since the last famine, which had brought many of these rather fearsome nomads into the town to settle. It was lovely to watch the sun set on the desert, and listen to the sounds. There were no engines. I could only hear the sounds of people and animals; children playing football, men and women chatting and making food, and goats bleating. The sounds carried a long way, as if it was over water. I took monkey out of my pocket, wound him up and set him going on the very top of the dune. He simply dug himself into a hole. I lay on my back, looking at the emerging stars, starting to sparkle in a pure, clear sky, - and then got frightened! I knew that many eyes would have followed me to my sandy perch, and it would be dark soon.

Although I had travelled a long way from Dakar, and had lots of character-building experiences, the old anxiety came back. I headed for the hotel. On the way back I was amazed at how many games of football were being played out in the desert. Every child in Timbuktu must play the game, mostly in bare feet. A huge area of sand, on the northern fringe of the town, had been levelled and turned into multiple football pitches, and they were all in use, however, bad light was about to stop play. There were no floodlights.

As my old mum would have said, it had been a *big* day since I had that morning cup of coffee on the boat, and I would have happily collapsed into bed, but I had promised to meet

Damien and Joanna in the Amanar to hear how they had got on at the Tuaregs' tent.

Damien had a tale to tell about the camel train. Out in the desert, they were told that the train had left only twenty minutes before, but Damien had spotted some camels a few dunes away, and thinking that this was the disappearing train, he told Joanna to follow, and sprinted off, hopefully to get a rear end photo. The old Tuareg guide who was with them was horrified and, try as he might, couldn't catch up. There were only about ten camels, but, convinced that this was *the* train, Damien started snapping from a distance, until he became aware that he was surrounded by young Tuaregs, demanding money. They pounced, and rifled every pocket, removing any loose change they found. At last, the guide caught up and, sweating and cursing, chased them.

"You took photos. You must pay!"

Oh, I could have told him that! Especially if it's a *train*.

Luckily, Damien had been wise, and most of his cash was hidden about his body where they couldn't reach, but he was shaken. I knew that feeling. To add insult to injury, when they had told the Amanar waiter about the incident, he laughed, and said that there hadn't been a camel train for weeks, and certainly not that day.

Then they had gone to the Tuareg tent but, by that time, were in no great mood to pay more money, so drank several cups of thick very strong tea, and bought no necklaces.

We all learn by our mistakes, or should.

After a couple of beers, and an exchange of addresses, I excused myself, and headed for bed, exhausted.

Jimmy was waiting for me.

As I entered the hotel yard I was stopped by this young African lad, probably no more than 14 years old, in jeans and Arsenal tee shirt.

"My name is Jimmy. You want a car to Mopti tomorrow?"

It took me a few seconds to catch up. I was still in the flush of excitement at being in Timbuktu, and my mind hadn't got round to thinking about leaving yet. I certainly wanted to stay at least one more day.

"No thanks. I'm staying a couple of days."

"But you want car. When do you want car? I get you car for day after tomorrow."

At least he spoke a bit of English, which made things easier.

"I might want a car the day after that, but *I* will decide when, thanks."

"OK, I get you car day after tomorrow. Twenty five thousand is cost."

"Listen, I haven't decided yet when I'm leaving, and anyway, twenty five thousand is too much. Twenty thousand, no more. I might get a better offer anyway. I'll decide later"

"Good, I come back tomorrow and we talk. You give deposit now."

"No. Good night Jimmy. I might see you tomorrow."

"OK mister, I come back tomorrow."

I lay, at last in bed.

Yes, a *big* day.

....

The next day was to have a special start. I was going to shave. There was even some hot water in the toilet. "This might take a while," I thought as I lathered the three day stubble, then took the first stroke. Nothing. Certainly, the foam came off my face as if a tiny little snow-plough had trundled across it, but the stubble field beneath was still all there, proud and erect. Considering that it was a brand new "Gillette" razor, and I had just un-wrapped the blade and inserted it, this was a puzzle. I tried again. Nothing. It was a dud! A very blunt Chinese apology for a razor. More a face scraper than a hair reaper. I didn't need my face scraped. I wanted a shave. I had been ripped off. All of 450 CFAs down the drain. Well that shop wasn't going to get my custom again! I wasn't going to let a thing like that get me down though, so I picked up monkey and headed to the roof for my first proper look at my surroundings.

Timbuktu is almost level, so although the roof gave me a bit of height, I could only really get a proper view of the adjoining buildings and yards. This was pretty good though. Next door was a large open compound with two Yurt type tents, and an inner pen of thorny branches containing a few goats. Apart from that there was only one small rough shelter at the far end of the compound. I imagined this was the toilet. Obviously, the Tuareg family that was living there hadn't fully committed to permanent town life. I couldn't blame them. Looking down into the yard of the hotel, I could see that Belli, and his family occupied one of the little out-buildings, where they obviously slept, ate and washed. Their bed was on the ground. The building was smaller than my bedroom.

Belli's wife was already washing bed linen.

Not far to the north, The Flamme de la Paix monument dazzled in the morning sun. As I took a time delay photo of my monkey and me with the monument behind us, I tipped a very small amount from my little bottle of Targemaker whisky into a cup, and drank to our success. Ok, it was early morning, but this was special. It might be my only full day in Timbuktu.

Getting there had been like climbing a mountain, and although I liked climbing mountains, there was one thing I hated - having to come down. At least I would have this day to savour.

From my vantage point, I could see people gathering in a wide flat area just to the north, and decided it needed a bit of investigation, so headed out to the sand past the monument. Tamimou, at the Amanar, just opposite, had told me that The Flamme de la Paix was built in 1996 to commemorate the end of an uprising by the Tuaregs, and that reputedly about 3,000 weapons had been burned, and buried in the concrete. Certainly part of the structure was a shallow dome set in the ground, with lots of rusty old rifles embedded in it. The monument itself defied me to write an accurate description. Rising up from four broad feet were two tall arches, joined together by a smaller arch, and there were also two flying buttresses, between the main arches, all covered in white tiles which shone out in the sun. Quite a few of the tiles were missing, and it was difficult to tell whether this was by design, fair wear and tear, or they had been nicked to decorate a tent or two. The arches were topped off with four open-work metal globes, perhaps representing the world. All in all I guessed it was about eighty feet high, and pretty imposing, though quite incongruous, stuck out on its own at the edge of the desert.

In fact this wasn't actually *The Desert.* This, I discovered, was the killing field. Little groups of people were gathering together with their goats, and a few cows, then splitting up again to re-convene further on. I realised that this was the animal market, and when I looked to the far edge of the area, saw that it was also the butchery. I had once been in a slaughterhouse in Britain, and the memory was not one I cherished, so when I saw the throat cutting in the sand, I turned away. I didn't need photos of that. I did notice though that there were also a couple of impromptu football matches taking place next to the slaughter.

I decided to change the taste in my mouth with a coffee, so headed into town. The Al Haat Patisserie and Restaurant had a ring-side view of one of the most colourful Timbuktu streets, and I spent a while just watching the women in multi-coloured African garb carrying their babies in shawls on their backs; the land cruisers loaded to over capacity with everything from bedding to timber; and the large herds of goats being driven to their fate.

This Patisserie was not the cool, plate-glass windowed type I had enjoyed in Bamako, but a large, squat, sky-blue concrete shed, with its open street side draped in heavy curtains to deter the heat and the flies, which in Timbuktu were legion. By pulling back a couple of curtains, I could see the view, and let the flies in. The coffee and cakes were good.

The Grand Marché was a two storey building housing numerous stalls, mostly of local produce for local consumption. Perhaps because Timbuktu is a small place without a huge tourist population, the market had no particular strangeness or *buzz* to it, and seemed to just function as the local supermarket. I did, however, tempt fate and buy two "Bic" disposable razors, which were being sold individually for some reason. I should have known better, but I was now *desperate* for a shave. Perhaps my continuing streaming cold was clouding my judgement, not to mention making my stubble an unsightly mess.

Thinking about my *date* with Kate, I set off south towards the internet café, praying that it would be open, and the young attendants awake. Although it was a good half hour's walk, I reckoned there was still time for a small detour, so popped into the Tourist office and got my passport stamped "TIMBUKTU". Wow!

This route took me past a big, quite modern secondary school. It was a-buzz with hundreds of teenagers on their break. Many of them were in beautiful traditional dress, but most were like teenagers anywhere, in jeans and tee-shirts. The thought struck me that while I was watching a thoroughly modern school scene right before me, goats were having their throats cut not far away in the desert sand. All part of life for these kids.

The whole of Timbuktu was like that – a mixture of the strictly traditional, and the very modern, with turbaned Tuaregs on camels jostling for space with bright young people driving 4x4s, and mud brick houses sporting satellite dishes on their roofs. There was even a small airport on the south west outskirts of town, where the more elite tourists could arrive for a few hours to see the Tuareg tents, and then escape back to the fleshpots of Bamako. I wondered what tensions might lie underneath such a diversity of cultures.

As for flying out – there would be no such easy escape for me. I still had Jimmy to contend with.

At the internet café all was calm of course, but I did seem to be recognised, and actually received a smile, which I returned with interest, reckoning that I should keep on the right side of the custodians of the only internet access in town.

My timing was good, and at exactly 12 noon, I logged on and sent a quick test email to see if Kate was there. It went wrong of course. Timbuktu internet connections were *very* slow, so by the time my message had reached Kate, she had sent one of her own. They crossed. They crossed again, but eventually we got in sync, and we were able to have a bit of a conversation, although pretty stilted, with me trying to concoct a reply to Kate's next question before it arrived, to save time. It was fun though, to think that we had a live link between Inverness and Timbuktu. Eventually it was time to finish, so I sent her my little *Pinasse Poem,* and said I'd try again tomorrow.

Since I was at the south end of the town, it seemed a good idea to carry on down the road to get a photo at the archway gate I had come through the day before in the Landrover.

It was a longer and sweatier walk than I had expected, since the gateway was right at the southern extremity of the town. It was worth it though. To have a photo of me standing under the big "Ville de Tombouctou" sign was what I had come all this way for. When I saw that it said "Tombouctou" not "Timbuktu", I realised that my mother had lied! What the hell, to me it will always be Timbuktu.

All I had to do now was walk all the way back to the Sahara Passion in the searing heat, *and have a shave*, but looking over to my right, I spotted something.

The town water tower was standing head and shoulders above the surrounding buildings, looking like something out of "War of the Worlds", and I remembered that the guide book had suggested that the best view of Timbuktu was from that very tower. Since it was so difficult to get a good perspective on the town any other way, I decided to go for it. Perhaps the heat was addling my brain, and making me forget recent train-station events, and although it may have been illegal to take a photo of a scrappy old train, surely there would be nothing wrong with an old lone white man climbing up the water supply tank of this small African town, and taking photos towards the army barracks. Who could object to that? Just to cover myself, I asked permission. In the open yard which housed the tower there was an old man on his knees on a mat, at his prayers and a little boy of about seven, sitting near him. I certainly didn't want to disturb anyone's prayers, so asked the boy if it would be ok for me to climb up this tower and take photos. He nodded, and said something completely unintelligible, which I interpreted as "Aye, ok." In retrospect, he may have said "Yes, and if you do, you'll probably be shot."

I was half-way up the ladder, which was already giving me exciting views, when I became aware of a screaming and screeching below me. It is not polite to disturb someone when they are communing with their god, and the old man was trying to explain this to me. He was emphasising the lesson by waving a rather ugly-looking stick, and, I supposed, claiming it was *his* tower. The memory of Kayes returned, and my blood ran cold. How long would it be before this old man's six strapping sons arrived to haul me off to the *polis*? I came down quickly, without a photo. At the bottom, I tried to explain by waving my arms expansively, making clicking motions with my camera, and smiling a lot. This appeared to enrage him more, so I did what I should have done earlier. *I ran.* Luckily he was much older than I was, and obviously chose not to kill himself by chasing me, but I had to hope he had little access to a phone, since I had a long way to go, and my route passed the police station, and the barracks.

I tried to saunter back through town, looking as if butter wouldn't melt, but all the time feeling that everyone was pointing and saying "Look, that's the old foreigner that climbed our tower. Go for the police!"

Nothing happened, and I found myself in a cemetery.

I didn't know it was a cemetery, just thought that it was a big area being prepared for housing – maybe some buildings had been demolished since there were lots of big loose stones, and bits of pots. I was about to wander about looking at the bits and pieces, when a very friendly young man rushed up and explained things. The stones were grave markers, the bits and pieces had sentimental value. I was walking on graves. I wasn't doing that day very well so headed for home.

Now I was going to have that shave! With *two* brand new razors I couldn't go wrong.

The first one was blunt. So what? I had another. It was blunt. I smothered a scream, and softly cursed Chinese imports for again dashing my hopes and dreams. I could not go on like this. It was shave, or die.

Deep in the bottom of my rucksack, I fished around, and lo and behold, found the broken head of my old *British* razor. Ok, it was just a little bar of plastic about an inch and a half long, but it had a blade embedded in it, and I knew that blade was *sharp*. With great difficulty considering that my hands were slippy, I caught it between thumb and forefinger, and carefully scraped it over my cheek. It worked! It worked! And very slowly, with many slips and drops, I de-fuzzed my face. By the end, I was exhausted, but exhilarated, and better still, exfoliated. It had taken twenty minutes, but ninety five per cent of my face was now *smooth*, leaving only a little impossible bit directly under my nose still hairy, and a bit itchy. Oh, I felt good. The day was looking up again and I reckoned that I could now survive without another shave till I got back to civilisation in Mopti, or wherever I got to when I left Timbuktu.

After a bit of a rest to recover from all the exertion, I was drawn back to the desert, and found myself on top of my favourite dune again. The familiar sounds of football, and people talking quietly, was soothing, so I lay back on the sand, surrounded by the Tuareg tents, and little groups of camels. Glancing round, I noticed a Tuareg youth passing the back of my dune and going into one of the tents. He came out a moment later carrying a huge curved knife, and seemed to be heading straight for me. I got a bit tense, but he veered off with a little smirk, and disappeared behind an adjacent dune. There was then a short burst of frantic bleating from some poor little goat, and I realised that *it* had been on the menu, not me.

I relaxed again, and lay, looking down the long, steep, corrugated side of the dune, at the scarab beetles which were starting to emerge. These were *big* black beetles, about an inch and a half long, and looked pretty fearsome as they scrambled up towards me, leaving long scalloped trails on the pristine face of the sand. I was sure they meant me no harm, but as each got within arm's-reach, I threw a handful of sand at it which knocked it back a foot or two. This didn't deter them, and they soon were beginning to overwhelm my position, so drastic action was needed. I took out a pencil I had brought with me to write a postcard, and *donked* the nearest beetle, batting it right down to the bottom of the dune. The "donk" noise each one made as I batted it was so satisfying, and so much fun, that I found myself giggling like an infant. This was a good game, and the poor little chaps didn't seem to be hurt or even mind so much. In fact, those that only went a short distance came back for more. I became so adept at this that I was able to write a couple of postcards, with only one eye on the beetles, and as any came near me, I would casually donk it away, and carry on writing.

The day ended with me drinking the last of my Targemaker whisky on top of the dune, and reciting my Pinasse Poem to the stars.

I had decided that the following day would be my last full day in Timbuktu. Although I was still enjoying being on my mountain, anxiety about finding my way back to Dakar, and home, was starting to grow.

I think I was falling in love with Timbuktu and the Sahara, and by 6.30 the next morning, I was already about two miles into the desert, sitting on top of the highest dune in the area. The town looked far away, and I sat for a long time just *being there*. This was not Scotland. This was nothing I had experienced before. This was just me, here, now. I knew that the sight, the sound and the experience would stay with me forever, and I didn't want to leave. But time was starting to get tight. It had taken me eleven days to get there from Dakar, and my flight home was in ten days' time. I had no plan yet how to get back. Nothing was booked and nothing could be relied on. I didn't even know yet how I would get out of Timbuktu. I had been told that for someone like me, a lone traveller, it could be easier to *get* there than to leave, and although I knew that might be true psychologically, I hoped that physically it wouldn't be that difficult. I was reasonably sure that Jimmy would soon appear and arrange transport for me. What could possibly go wrong? I spent a little while longer writing a couple more postcards, then headed back to town, promising the desert that I would return to see my last sunset.

In a little café near the Petit Marché, I had a Nescafé amid a noisy swarm of flies, and when an old stooped Tuareg approached me and asked if there was anything I wanted to buy, I took pity and asked if he had any postcards.

"No, but I will get one for you," and he sent a small boy hurrying away towards the market. I wasn't sure whether he was being very obliging, or was simply desperate, but decided no matter what the price was (within reason), I would buy his postcard. The little boy soon came panting back and handed the card to the old man, with a smile. I was surprised. Although the card looked as if it had been around for a while, it was rather nice, with a picture of a typical Timbuktu house, complete with donkey, and *he only asked 250 CFAs for it*. This was no rip off, he was simply being helpful. I gave the man 500, and the little lad 250, and we were all happy. That postcard was not going to be posted, but would travel home with me. However, I did need more than one, so I popped into the post office on the way to the internet café, and got a supply, all at the same price as the old man had asked.

Trying to send emails was a nightmare. The connection still kept shutting down, and when it did work, was abysmally slow. The two lads running the place simply shrugged. I guessed that to them, a rubbish internet connection was better than no internet connection. After half an hour I had only managed to send one short message to my daughters, with a copy to Kate, so I gave up, in the hope that the next day I would be somewhere more "connected".

Heading back to the hotel, I decided to meander a bit, and take in bits of the old part of town that I hadn't really looked at before. I knew that there were a couple of famous houses, where early European explorers had stayed in the

1800s. There was also a mosque that my guide book said I could enter. I was going to do the tourist thing.

Once I had found someone to pay for entry into the Djingueribar Mosque (I wasn't going to repeat my water-tower experience), I was free to wander through it on my own. The only stipulation was that I should take off my shoes, and be respectful. It was empty, apart from me, and was like being in a huge hangar, with rows on rows of massive columns holding up a high roof. The floor was almost totally covered in small individual carpets, each one owned by an individual worshipper, and as I stood in the middle of this massive building, I could almost *hear* the silence. A feeling of complete calm flowed through me, and I could have stayed for the whole day. Sitting there for an hour, with my back to a pillar in the middle of this wonderful sanctuary possibly changed my whole being for ever, but eventually some locals came in and broke the spell, so it was out and onward for me. I veered over towards the east of the town, managing to see the couple of old explorers' houses, from the outside. They were not impressive, and but for the plaques on their walls, were just like all the others – mud-brick, with a sand floor. I didn't attempt to go into them, but contented myself with peering through the doors.

The more I wandered through Timbuktu, the more I liked it. It had a reputation for being boring. I found it anything but. The people were mostly polite and welcoming, and actually smiled as I passed them. Perhaps they were starting to recognise this wee grey haired white man, with a penchant for climbing water towers.

It was now time to buy a few souvenirs. They had to be small since I still had a long way to travel, so I decided on some rather nice Tuareg necklaces in the "Maison des Artisans" which was on the way back to the Sahara Passion. The artisans who were trading in this dark little market were quite insistent, but not aggressively so, and I enjoyed a bit of banter with them. Three necklaces later, we were all smiles and happy.

Back at the hotel, I met Karim, a young Canadian who had "gone native" for a couple of months, and had lived with the Tuaregs in the desert, travelling extensively by camel. He was now going to have a rest at the Sahara Passion before going on to where he did not know. Meeting people like him and Jacques was invigorating and although I could never compete with them in the adventure stakes, I did feel that I was a little part of that fraternity.

A sardine lunch in my room tasted delicious, but was disturbed by Belli knocking at the door.

"Please come and talk to a man about transport."

The man turned out to be Caleel, a youth of about sixteen who said he was "The boss of the Association".

"I get you transport. 20,000 in front, 15,000 in back."

He didn't say of what, and I had visions of an Alham.

"OK, I could be interested, but what about Jimmy? He was supposed to meet me."

"Jimmy will see you tonight in the restaurant, and make plans with you."

"Right, but remember, I will only pay once I am in the car."

My mother always told me never to pay anything for a bargain on the doorstep, especially before you've got your hands on it. She was from Glasgow. I finished my lunch then dozed, wondering what the return journey back to Dakar would bring. The nerves were starting to tickle my stomach.

Later, perched on top of my little sand mountain, I spent a couple of lovely lazy hours waiting for my last Timbuktu sunset, watching groups of camels being brought together and traded in the sand, and listening to the now familiar sounds of the desert. I didn't want to come down, but the pressure was mounting. I knew I must soon leave my mountain. As the sparkling clear sky turned grey then black, speckled with a myriad of piercingly sharp diamonds, I reluctantly slid down the steep side of the dune and dragged my heels towards the Amanar and Jimmy.

He arrived during my Spag Boll, which I wasn't really enjoying anyway. The thought of leaving was making me morose. I really did like the place.

The deal, according to Jimmy, was 25,000 CFAs for front seats, 22,500 for middle, and 15,000 for back seats. I corrected him to Caleel's figures, but said I would take a back seat at 15,000 anyway. Perhaps my mood was clouding my judgement, but I should have wondered why the back seats were so much cheaper. I didn't even ask if it would be a 4x4 or a camel.

Jimmy then asked for a deposit.

"Not on your life. I'll pay when I see the car – no – when I'm *in* the car."

"OK, then can you give me a tee-shirt?"

"What? Away to Timbuktu! At this moment, you've probably got more tee-shirts than I have! Anyway, what time will the car come for me in the morning? I don't want an early start."

"The car will be about ten or eleven. You must be ready."

Now, that was just what I wanted to hear. I would have a nice long lie and a leisurely breakfast before the trip.

"OK, see you then." and I gave him a 1,000 CFA note.

I had to experience Timbuktu one last time, so walked slowly through the town, my hands deep in my pockets, my mind deep in my mood.

In the bright crystal moonlight the town is carpeted in snow. Tall dark people walk silently through the streets. Little children play in the deep drifts, and laughter rings out as semi-circles of squatting Tuaregs watch television football from far-away places. There is no traffic, and overhead, in the endless black sky, the silence is heaven. There are no planes to force their way with noise and flame through the stars.

Little Christmas donkeys stand quietly in the snow, close under the trees, and men approach to offer a trip to the desert. In the moonlight they look fierce, but only want to sell a necklace, or a long knife.

Small warm circles of lights from fires and lamps stud the alleyways, and the main streets are like ice rinks in the harsher glare of the traders' little neon strips. Where the snow is hard packed by the four by fours, it crinkles and cracks underfoot.

People say "Ca va?" quietly as they pass in this dark town of snow and a hundred strange musics spill softly out of canvas doors onto the drifts which pile right up to the houses, and into them.

Two hundred men suddenly appear from everywhere, and quietly, intently, join and walk towards their God. It is private.

There is a kind of innocence that you can only experience when it snows softly, late at night.

In the morning, the bright sun will light the snow, and turn it back to sand. It is magic.

At six in the morning the magic was gone and Belli was hammering on my door.

Six o'clock! I had set my alarm for eight.

"Mister. Mister. Jimmy is here."

I couldn't believe it. It was still dark and I was now in a different kind of mood.

"Mister, Jimmy says come quick. The car will leave."

I struggled into my trousers and headed for the gate where Jimmy seemed to be aghast that I wasn't fully geared up and ready to go.

"Jimmy, you said ten, or eleven. It's only six, for God's sake!"

There was a 4x4 sitting in the street, its engine running, and the driver staring straight forward.

"Please, you must come. The car is going now."

"Jimmy, NO. I was asleep, and you said ten or eleven. If you give me half an hour to eat and get ready ok, but I'm not ready now."

At that, the driver revved up, said something which was probably quite rude to Jimmy, and sped off. Jimmy now seemed distraught, and said that there would be no other cars that day, but Belli, hearing this, chased him, apparently calling him a lying little brat, or the local equivalent.

Through Karim, who was now up to see what was going on, Belli told me that if I went to the Gare Routier at the Grand Marché later on, I would surely get a car out. He assured me that I certainly didn't need a guide just to get a car.

So much for my long lie, but by now I was mentally prepared to tackle the trip, so got my stuff together and headed into town for a coffee-and-bun breakfast. I dithered in the café, spinning out my last little while in Timbuktu, but eventually had to go and look for transport down my mountain.

The Grand Marché was strangely quiet, but there was an old bus there, and a couple of 4x4s, so I asked in the nearest shop where I could get a ticket, or seat in a car.

"Sorry mister, there is nothing going out today. The bus will go tomorrow."

Ah.

"Are you sure? I was told there would be cars today."

"They've all gone, very early. Try the Tourist Office. Perhaps they can help you."

So I wasn't panicked yet. I had plenty options. After all, it seemed that *everyone* would be happy to take my money for the trip.

At the Tourist Office the guy was very sympathetic, and said that he would arrange a car, and I should come back at noon. I got the impression that there was something he wasn't telling me.

Now I had some time to kill, which suited fine since I really was dragging my heels anyway. I walked to the local bank to change some sterling and my remaining Travellers' Cheques.

"Sorry sir, we only deal in American Express. I can't help you." and he looked straight in my eye, without a smile. That seemed quite unfriendly.

On the chance that I might be able to arrange things myself, I visited the Boctou Hotel, and asked the old receptionist if he knew of a car heading out. Without looking up he said that there was –"*Tomorrow*", and he emphasised "*At six in the morning*" then went back to his book. I was now starting to feel that I was getting the cold shoulder, and it wasn't from the weather, even though I had noticed that people in the street were wearing jackets and jumpers. A wind had risen, swirling a fine dust through the streets and taking yesterday's razor-sharp edge off the horizons.

Ok, if Jimmy had put it round that I was "Persona non Grata" I didn't care. I'd get a car at the Tourist Office and be off and away. Definitely no tee-shirt for Jimmy now!

I was now *kicking* my heels, and was relieved when twelve o'clock arrived and could head off. I was ready to leave. The office was closed.

By twelve forty-five, I had got the message. I wasn't going to be going. Not that day.

A little knot started to tighten in my stomach. What if I didn't get a car tomorrow? Or the next day? They had me over a barrel, and I couldn't get any money out of the bank. I could be in a fix. Surely not *everyone* would be against me. Was I becoming paranoid?

I felt too embarrassed to go back to The Sahara Passion, so, tail between my legs, I again approached the receptionist in the Boctou.

"Sorry, we have no rooms tonight."

"*What?*"

"You can sleep on the roof. 6,000."

"Ah, Thanks."

The hotel was only two floors high, so finding my *bed* was pretty easy. The roof was actually quite a good spot, if you don't mind sleeping on concrete. Perhaps that's not fair. There *were* several six-inch-thick foam mattresses lying around, so I took my pick and set up camp with my back to the wall of the stair- well. With *my* foam mattress on top of *their* foam mattress, my sleeping bag on top of that, and my rucksack as a pillow, it looked positively idyllic.

Looking down from the quite ornate pierced concrete block wall around the edge of the roof, I could see, pitched in the middle courtyard, four small backpackers' tents. That was obviously one stage up from sleeping on the roof, but the view wasn't so good. Outside of the hotel, the wind was beginning to stir the sand a bit more, and things were becoming hazy, but there was no masking the areas strewn with years of litter. Even though it was near the middle of town, the hotel was surrounded by Tuareg tents and encampments, and on one side were the collapsed remains of the old town water well – a huge circular pit that had once been lined with bricks. It was now half filled with sand. Alongside it was an area covered in hundreds of drying mud bricks. As I looked down on a hazy scene of a little circle of local boys, sitting playing some game in the sand, with their camel "charges" tethered to a scrubby tree alongside them, I heard a noise on the other side of the stairwell.

Anna appeared. She was a young German girl, who had good English, and she proceeded to set up a double camp on the other side of the stairwell. She explained that her boyfriend Peter was travelling in Africa for a year, and she had joined him for the Mali part of his trip. It appeared that sleeping on a roof in the middle of Timbuktu was no great problem for her as she set about *making house*. Peter was off doing the shopping. It all seemed so easy for that generation. For my part, I was starting to feel a bit weary.

I headed downstairs and paid my dues to the grumpiest receptionist in Africa

(I *have* met worse on the west coast of Scotland)

Now, 6,000 CFAs lighter, and with my head hanging a bit, I slouched out into the sunlight, looking for a beer, and immediately several guides started offering me a lift to Mopti the next morning! It was impossible to tell if they were vying with each other, or working together, and I became so disorientated that I threw my hands up in the air and shouted "Stop!"

Then, looking straight at the biggest of them, I said "I will be here at six tomorrow morning. If you are here with a car, and will take me and my bag to Mopti, I will give you 20,000 CFAs. I will pay you when I am in the car. If you are not here at six, I will go with one of these people," and smiled at the others.

"Ok, there will be no problem."

"Aye, we'll see," I thought, and scurried back into the hotel.

"How much for a large beer, please?" to the receptionist.

"1250."

That was twice the going rate, and I wasn't going to pay it.

"Ok, how much for a small beer?"

"750."

I capitulated.

"A small beer please."

"We only have large."

To hell with that! I wasn't going to pay those prices.

My throat was parched, and was getting worse with the swirling dust as I made my way to The Poulet D'Or in the Maison des Artisans, where surely the prices would be sensible, and I would get a better welcome.

"Sorry, we do not serve beer, but if you want I will send my son to get a bottle for you."

I inwardly screamed, thanked the waiter, and left.

The Colomb Hotel, near to the Boctou, was by comparison, up-market, and although I had decided that it was bound to be too dear, I was now desperate and had floating visions of a long cool beer on its roof top bar, as I trudged back up the sand street, litter swirling around me.

"A small beer please."

"1,000 CFAs please."

Ach, you've got to give in sometime.

I took my glass, and moved a chair to the edge of the roof, to watch the action below.

"Sorry sir, you cannot sit there."

"*What?*" The place was empty apart from me, and surely I wasn't taking someone else's spot. There must be a Timbuktu mafia, and a contract had been put out on me to make my last few hours in town as uncomfortable and expensive as possible. If I ever meet Jimmy again ....

Then, an angel, in the shape of the head waiter appeared and assured me that where I was would be ok, but would I please not make it too obvious that I was drinking alcohol. It seemed that he was non Mafiosi, and actually smiled at me. Half an hour later, my throat a bit slicker, and my mood more relaxed, it was time to try the internet to let Kate know of my plight. Jimmy must have got there first. The connection was virtually dead and no matter how I tried, my messages wouldn't go through. Even the internet was ganging up on me. The boys again just shrugged their shoulders. It really was time to get out of Timbuktu.

Back at the door of the Boctou, yet another young guy approached me.

"My name is Toré. I can get you a car tomorrow, to take you to Mopti."

"Toré, my friend," I said, placing my hand on his shoulder as gently as I could, considering my urge to strangle him "You are now the fifth person today to make that offer. I really don't know who will be taking me tomorrow, but I do feel that you are maybe all just trying to wind me up. I will be here at six o'clock, and whoever takes me first, gets paid.

"I will be here. Goodbye."

Minutes later, as I was sorting out my things on the roof, Toré reappeared, with Mohammed.

"This man will be your driver tomorrow. 20,000 CFAs with bag. Six o'clock. Goodbye."

"Fine, Goodbye."

Surely, surely, *someone* would take me tomorrow. Surely.

Although I was too embarrassed to go back and say another farewell to Belli, I did decide that I wanted a last, last meal in the Amanar, where Tamimou had been so friendly.

Tamimou was surprised to see me, but seemed pleased. Over a beer, I explained my plight, and he sympathised, agreeing that in a place the size of Timbuktu, it is unwise to tread on anyone's toes. Since the restaurant was still very quiet, he sat with me and we chatted about my life, and his plans. He hoped that the Amanar would become *the* place in Timbuktu, but felt he needed to do more to attract the small number of tourists that visited the town. NGO staff and business people already came, but the tourists tended to be shepherded into the hotels. I suggested that fairy lights and "Tuareg theme nights" as per Mediteranean restaurants might help. He laughed, and said it was a nice idea but perhaps would be a bit out of place. One of his main hopes was that the "Festival au Desert", a music festival held about 40 kilometres North of Timbuktu, each January, would build up and become more and more famous. It already brought a large number of visitors through Timbuktu, but only for a short time, and most of them were African. He really wanted to attract more Westerners. I assured him that since he was such an enthusiastic charismatic guy, he would definitely succeed, and become rich and famous, but he said he had some grave fears. Pointing to the Flamme de la Paix monument, he reminded me that it wasn't long since the Tuaregs had last rebelled.

"If the government keeps them sweet, and keeps the army strong, we will have peace, but if the Tuaregs rise again, no tourists will come. Like you, I do not come from here, so I will have to flee back to Togo, if I can."

We talked on for a while, then, when business associates arrived, he gave me a beer, and joined them in conference. I really hoped that all would go well for him, and as I left, I wished him luck. As far as I could see, the Tuaregs seemed happy enough, but what did I know?

On the roof of the Boctou, I had a short chat with Anna and Peter, and apologised in advance for possibly waking them early the next day at six, as I left.

Setting my alarm for 5.00 a.m., I settled down to gaze at a beautiful, but hazy sky, and listen to some Timbuktu tots playing ball somewhere below. With so many people now wanting to take me, I was pretty sure that I would be leaving the next day. It had to be. I had a long way to go and time was getting short.

I closed my eyes for the last time in Timbuktu.

9. COMING DOWN THE MOUNTAIN

At three in the morning, *three in the morning,* the call to prayer rang out, not from some far away mosque, but from a loudspeaker attached to a post about ten feet from the side of the hotel. It was *loud.* Then others started up, a bit further away, but just as loud. It seemed that the Imam of each mosque was trying to outdo the others. Our one was certainly holding his own, and if it hadn't been *three in the morning,* I might have cheered him on. As it was, I wasn't in the mood. The calls then went on like this, lasting about five minutes, every half hour for the next two hours.

It was a not so subtle form of torture.

Five minutes' hollering - awake. Ten minutes trying to doze off again - half asleep. Fifteen minutes quiet -fitful sleep. Then CALL TO PRAYER, again.

I could then appreciate how the typical Malian seemed to have an amazing capacity for sleep during the day. They're not allowed to sleep at night! I had not been aware that this was happening every day in the middle of town, since obviously, the distance of the Sahara Passion from the action and its thick mud walls had dulled the message enough to let me sleep through.

"At least," I thought, "I'll be ready this time for the car," and at about 4.45 crept downstairs to wash and prepare myself for the day. I don't know why I *crept,* when the whole world must have been awake by then. With lots of time to prepare, I slowly and carefully packed up, and was just about to sit by the wall for one last ponder when the door to the stairs burst open and Toré was there.

"Ok. We go. *Now!*"

So much for me being in charge and choosing my transport at six o'clock.

A quick "Bye" to Peter and Anna, who of course were wide awake, then I was bundled into the back of a 4x4 alongside two Africans. There was lots of commercial-looking gear in the boot. This was obviously not a *tourist* trip. I was baggage. Almost immediately we were off, but soon stopped at a fairly smart local house, where a woman was helped into the front seat, and her wheelchair was squeezed into the boot. At first I thought that she was the mother of one of the men, but discovered that she was a nurse in the hospital at Timbuktu, and was travelling to Bamako for treatment herself. I reckoned that she was probably the main paying passenger, and I was subsidising her fare. OK by me. I was heading home.

On the way to the ferry, I tried to ask the driver if he would take me as far as Segou, since I really fancied the luxury of "The Auberge" again.

"Yes, ok. It will be another 70,000 CFAs."

"Oh. ok, No, I'll just get off at Mopti thanks."

"We are not going to Mopti. We will drop you at Sevaré. You will get a taxi from there."

It seemed that I certainly was not in control of this trip in any way at all. Who knows, if I had waited till six, at the door, I might have got a better deal. Then again, perhaps I would still be there at ten. Anyway, all was not lost. Sevaré was on the main route to Bamako, only a few miles east of Mopti, and my book told me that there was a place called "Mac's Refuge" there, which sounded intriguing, and got good reviews. If it turned out to be a hole, I could still get a bus to Segou, or into Mopti, if there was one. I had no idea when we might get to Sevaré, so planning was difficult, and the driver simply waved both his hands in the air when I asked him for an ETA.

"Ok. Sevaré is fine. Thanks."

The sun was just rising when we got to the ferry at Korioumé, and I realised why we had been in such a rush to get there early. The ferry takes about three large vehicles and very little else. The crossing isn't just a simple case of going across the Niger. Various islands and inlets have to be negotiated, and the whole thing takes about thirty minutes. I saw only one ferry boat, and reckoned that if we had missed the first crossing, we would have been left sitting watching the ducks for an hour, and there were no ducks. It was only when we were on the ferry that the feeling crept up on me that I was coming off my mountain, and would probably never climb it again. A panoply of images rushed through my mind, and a little knot of regret tightened in my stomach. If I could have, I would have gone back for one more day. To my fellow passengers I must have seemed like a surly, silent Westerner, but they didn't feel as I felt. To them, this was normal life, just another journey: to me, anything but.

Once across, there was no hanging about, and we headed off on a red dust road through the scrubby desert. Since I was sitting next to a back window, I was getting quite a few mouthfuls of the red stuff, so started to wind it up a bit.

"Please leave the window open. It will be very hot." from the driver.

All the others seemed to agree, and being the odd-one-out in more ways than one, I had to grin, and literally swallow it. Luckily, my sunglasses at least protected my eyes.

It wasn't a smooth ride. Most of the time we were on what could be called a "graded dirt road", but every so often we hit a patch which was like driving over corrugated iron - at fifty miles an hour. It's not comfortable, and your teeth fall out, so we had to divert onto the sand, and crawl carefully along until we could get back onto a relatively smooth part. The first stop after an hour and a half was at a police point at Bambara. We were making good time, though sometimes a little fast for me, but perhaps the others wanted home again that night. Occasionally, like a scene from an American mid-West movie, a huge truck would appear through the haze ahead of us, and seem to hang in mid-air on the heat shimmer, as it grew and grew in size. Again, we would take to the sand. Luckily I had taken a big bottle of water with me, since that same red sand was now starting to cake my lungs.

Near Douentza, the countryside began to change, and beautiful jaggy mountains appeared through the mist. Some were like hands sticking abruptly up out of the desert, and it would have been easy to imagine that they held some spiritual force.

For a mountain boy, it was good to see, after spending so long in a flat landscape, and I watched, entranced, as camel riders, in traditional costumes, drove huge herds of cattle and goats towards the towns.

Once on the main tarmac highway at Douentza, we fair skelped along, and before I knew it, I was out, and on my own again at the Sevaré Gare Routier.

I was travelling again.

Before I attempted to find "Mac's Refuge", which I knew would be a taxi ride away, I visited the bus station and bought a ticket for the early bus to Bamako the next day. It would be another unearthly early start, but I was keen to reach Bamako with time to get my bearings for the next leg to Dakar. I was feeling a bit panicky in case the timing went wrong. There were eight days till my flight home, and I still hadn't decided how to do the Bamako to Dakar leg. I attracted quite a few stares, and a couple of giggles in the bus station, which I put down to me being *strange*. Again, I was the only "white" around, but it was only when I went into the toilet, where there was a rather hazy mirror on the wall, that I discovered that it was nothing to do with me being white. It had everything to do with me being *red*. My whole top half was covered in red dust. My mop of grey hair was now a bright Irish red. My face looked like the face of a very unwell communist panda (red face, white eyes), and my clothes sprayed red dust when I moved. *No one had told me.* I looked ridiculous, and I was sure my fellow passengers from Timbuktu were still giggling. There was nothing I could do. Since there was no water in the toilet, and anyway, to attempt to wash myself in a sink would have probably resulted in me being covered in red mud, rather than dust. I shook myself, and went looking for a taxi. The taxi driver didn't seem to notice anything odd about me, but perhaps that was because both he, and his taxi, were dirtier than I was.

Mac's Refuge, from the outside was daunting, and I almost turned away. It appeared to be a small prison, with fifteen foot high brick walls all round, punctuated by steel-shuttered windows, and I could just see what appeared to be a lookout tower over the top. Around about there were a few trees, at the edge of the wide red-dust street, and quite a lot of rubble. A herd of goats was grazing on one side. If I had thought that I was going to have a night of luxury, it looked like I might be mistaken, so I asked the taxi driver to hover for a bit.

I rang the bell at the high, wide blue gate, and was greeted by a stately old African.

"Hello, do you have a room for tonight?"

His eyes widened, ever so slightly, and then with one of the most welcoming grins I had seen in a long time, he said, "Yes, of course, sir. Please come in."

I paid the taxi driver, and then entered a different world.

Mac's Refuge was just that, a refuge from all that was outside those high *prison* walls. There was a lovely plant and flower-filled courtyard, a raised eating area with a huge wooden table, soft seating, and *a swimming pool*! Ok, it was perhaps even a little smaller than the one on top of the Independence in Dakar, but it was clean, and appeared to be devoid of aquatic bugs. It was also circular, and looked oh, so appealing. I took all this in, as I followed John through the courtyard and into a small corridor ending in a bedroom.

"I hope this room will do you, sir. Would you like me to wash your clothes?"

I could hardly believe my ears. Not once did he say "You're filthy." He simply offered to make me human again. I started to think I might just stay there for the rest of the trip!

"Oh, yes, please, and could you wash some others too, please?" I simpered.

"Certainly sir, just bring them to me when you're ready, and I'll have them washed and dried for tomorrow."

Was this Heaven? The room certainly looked like it could be. There was a soft bamboo-frame bed covered in an ornate multi-coloured cloth, mosquito net, curtains, *electricity and air conditioning*. It was even decorated with Tuareg wall hangings, and the paint was not flaking. It didn't have *facilities* though, but I soon found them along the corridor, and they were of the highest standard I had experienced in many days. There was running water. *Hot and cold.*

It is difficult to adequately describe the pleasure of stripping off all my smelly, dusty, stained clothes, and standing under that beautiful shower as the red dust turned to mud, then slid off me, leaving at last simple plain skin. I stood there for long minutes after I was clean as a baby, and simply luxuriated. My hair was grey again. My body was pink, and I was happy. I smiled to myself, then was unable to smother a little laugh of pleasure.

Oh boy. It took me much longer than it should have to sort my stuff out, I was enjoying it so much. I was clean, there was no rush, and I was in a safe place.

John was all smiles as I presented him with an armful of dirty linen, and he suggested that I might like a dip in the pool, though he did visually check me over for red dust before he said this, and seemed satisfied. He explained that, no, he wasn't "Mac", but had been Mac's employee for some time, and was in charge while his boss was away. Mac, in fact would be back later in the afternoon, when I would meet him. Meanwhile, I was welcome to use all the facilities, and by the way, would I like some lunch?

This place just got better and better. I had imagined that lunch would be the usual omelette and chips, but no, a delicious soup was followed by a plate of excellent Spaghetti Bolognese and finished with a mouth-watering melon dessert. This was *real* food, and even the beer which accompanied it seemed better than usual. I was in the middle of Mali, and I was "dining".

Later, I learned what it is like to be a goldfish. Since the pool was round, I swam continuously in a circle till I could swim no more. This was the first time I had swum since Segou, nine dusty, sweaty days before. It felt like I was flying, but all too soon I had to come to Earth, and realised that there were other things needing done.

I hadn't been in touch with Kate since before I left Timbuktu and she now wouldn't know where I was, so an internet café would be handy. I would also have to stock up with a few victuals, including cough sweets (my cold was now *in my chest)* for the bus the next day, since it would be a nine hour journey starting at 7.00 a.m. God, I would have to get up *again* at an unearthly hour and submit myself to never-ending travel. Although I felt quite relaxed now, and reckoned that my return to Dakar would be easy and trouble free, the timing was important, and the sooner I got to Bamako, the more options I would have from there on.

I dressed in the remaining third of my clothes, wishing that I had asked John to wash my trainers too, and stepped out to explore Sevaré.

Sevaré is a fairly big, stretched-out place, and since I didn't have a map, I had to follow my nose, but not get too adventurous. Eventually I came upon a bank, but it was shut. Then, a hotel, but the internet wasn't working so I had a beer. Perhaps it was my happy mood after a great lunch, a swim, and a couple of beers, but I wasn't bothered. Things would get better. I seemed to be near the middle of town, so decided that I had gone far enough, probably further than I should, and was about to head back to Mac's when I spotted a really colourful and interesting sight. At a junction, just alongside the edge of the street, there were thirty-four women (I counted them) in two rows, pounding maize with large wooden poles, all in unison, all wearing the most beautiful multi-coloured flowing clothes, and all singing some happy traditional song. This was not a tourist attraction. This was just what they did.

I *was* a tourist. I took a photo.

Immediately, they stopped, and almost as one, they turned and started shouting at me. I could tell from their gestures that they thought I was a bit rude, and should go away. Ok, I agreed with them, and if I had been brave enough, I would have gone over and apologised, but, come on, there were thirty-four of them, and they seemed a bit angry. I backed off, to a corner at a safe distance and took a few more long-distance shots. I was a tourist after all.

On the way back to Mac's, I followed the dual carriageway in the non-light of the usual huge street lamps. It seemed the straightest, safest route, although I had to negotiate my way past a huge herd of cattle being driven along it by two small boys. There was of course no traffic, and the dual carriageway ended abruptly just before Mac's.

John "Mac" McKinney turned out to be a larger-than-life big American with a beard and an even bigger welcome. He greeted me as if I was a long-time friend, and sat me down for a chat. He wanted to hear all about my travels and seemed genuinely interested in what I had achieved. He was kind. Mac had been born not far away, and knew every nook and cranny for many miles around. Timbuktu was in his back yard, but he was interested that I had been there. Eventually I got a bit of his story.

He was the son of an American missionary, and was born not far from Sevaré. He went to America for education, and returned, married, as a missionary, but when his marriage failed, he was told he could no longer be part of that church, so opened "Mac's Refuge". Mac McKinney was a warm, friendly, resourceful gentleman, who will always be a missionary, church or not. His Refuge catered mostly for NGO workers, other missionaries, and the occasional lonesome traveller like myself. We sat and chatted for a while, and then he invited me to join him for supper. He explained that it was Thanksgiving, and he had a few friends coming for a big meal. I was the only paying guest that night, and he didn't want to see me sitting on my own. It would be free. I explained to him that since I had a cough which would irritate everyone else at the table, and had a stomach which had started burbling alarmingly, and had to get out of bed at the crack of dawn, I *very* reluctantly would have to decline his offer, but wished him, and his guests a happy Thanksgiving. Mac accepted my little speech, but then sat me down again, and over the next half hour, filled me full of whisky. When I left him to his celebration, and clawed my way back to my room, I was euphoric, if that's the right word for it. Little did I know.

As I struggled to set my alarm, I convinced myself that Mac had promised to order a taxi for me at 6.30 the next morning.

I slept very deeply.

10. HOLD ON TIGHT

Considering the state I was in the night before, I woke at 6.00 a.m. with an amazingly clear head. Of course, I had been in a self-induced coma for almost ten hours, and the bed had been more comfortable than I'd had for quite a while. First thing to do was locate my washed, *and ironed* clothes, and I didn't have far to look as they were neatly folded on a chair outside my room. This really was a special place!

Once I was packed up and ready to go, I found James, the night watchman, quietly sweeping the courtyard.

"Good morning sir. Would you like coffee and some bread before you go?"

"Yes please. Do you know if Mac ordered a taxi for me?"

"I think so sir. Please sit."

Everything normal. Everything good.

The first sip of coffee hit a spot in my stomach which I didn't know existed, and my stomach groaned. The old familiar burbling started, and I felt a little shiver of unease caress the back of my neck. By the time I had finished the coffee and the bread, it was 6.30, and my stomach was in overdrive. My cold had also kicked in for the day, which was now rapidly losing its early charm. James suggested that we should open the gate a little so that we would know when the taxi arrived, but by 6.45 it still wasn't in sight. I panicked, and with James' help, phoned the taxi man who sounded surprised that I wanted him *now*. He assured me he would be there in "two minutes", so with a bit more confidence, I wished James goodbye, and he shut the gate, leaving me gazing up the long dusty road, as my stomach started to have a party again. I coughed.

And farted at the same time.

And my whole life came to a standstill.

I had had what my mother would have called "A little accident"!

Now, standing outside the *locked* gate of the only place that had facilities fit enough to deal with this emergency, I saw the dust of the taxi approaching and stood rooted to the spot, cold and incredulous. There was a nine hour bus journey ahead of me, and I had just had "A little accident".

And the taxi was coming.

It was only another fart that brought me to my senses and found me battering on the gate. Ok, if it woke Mac up, it served him right! His whisky had played a major part in this! Luckily, James was close, but was pretty surprised when I squeezed past him and headed for the toilet.

"Need toilet! Need toilet! Tell taxi to wait. Five minutes."

In only four minutes, I managed to strip, have the quickest shower I've ever had, flush and dispose of a pair of unsavoury underpants (leaving me with only two pairs), re-dress, repack, leave my glasses behind and take three Diacalm. The taxi driver drew *me* a look for not being ready, after I had demanded *his* presence, but that didn't bother me. What did bother me was the fact that my stomach had not improved just because I had had a shower, and was threatening to fart again.

I again thanked James, and walking with stiff legs, made it to the taxi. God, how was I going to survive the day? *Nine hours* and then I would have to try to get from the bus station to the hotel at the other end. And that bus station was *Bamako* bus station. I remembered the scene. God help me. I clenched every muscle in my body, till it settled again, and suddenly we were there. I hadn't noticed the two mile trip. I was far too absorbed in my "inner being".

There had, after all, been no rush. The bus was running late, but not so late that I had time to visit the primitive toilet block, so I found a double seat near the back of the bus, thankfully to myself, and settled in with a siege-like attitude. *I would not be moved.* I hoped.

Things almost went wrong before we even started, when I looked out the window and saw that I was opposite the bus station restaurant. On the ground outside its door, a woman and a couple of kids were cooking something in a large pot over an open fire. This was just below my window, and at the sight of the food, my stomach remembered the tin of tuna which I had bought the day before, for the journey, and revolted.

NO! Again, every muscle tightened, and as the bus moved off, the muscles won. Round two to me. I couldn't bear to remember round one.

Thus began the most difficult, uncomfortable bus journey of my life. Oh, the bus was comfortable enough, though old. No, it was me, wholly me. Every blip of my stomach was a crisis. Every bounce of the bus was a threat. Every cough could be disaster. And the bus went slowly, so slowly. I managed to divert my thoughts by concentrating on the many police check points, where thankfully, I wasn't asked to leave the bus, or even stand up, and the roadside Moped Garages, where the petrol pumps were simply racks of old water bottles filled with petrol. I supposed that they would come in very handy if Mali ever had another insurrection. There were many stops for prayers, and I drew a few looks, as I sat alone on the bus, in splendid isolation. I wasn't moving (in more ways than one) if I could help it. I just prayed for the *bus* to move.

And then the bus broke down.

It broke down alongside a row of roadside food stalls, and the driver said we would all have to get off. As I stepped down from the bus, first one, then all of the vendors beckoned to me to try their wonderful food. I was sure it would be delicious, but just managed to get past them, indicating exaggeratedly that I was oh, so full up, and escaped to a large boulder further down the road, where again, I sat stock still.

The day was not getting better.

Eventually, after spending quarter of an hour watching every other passenger from the bus poking and prodding at the engine, even *I* was tempted to look and see if *I* could tell what was wrong. Carefully, gingerly, I made my way through the little crowd, and reached the bus just as someone discovered a broken fan belt lying in the bottom of the engine compartment. There actually seemed to be several fan belts on the engine, but where this one should have been, there were only two shiny wheels. Problem solved. Not quite. I couldn't follow much of what was being said but gathered that someone would have to go for another belt. Where? How long would it take? I had no idea, and retreated back past the food stalls to my stone where I took my last Diacalm. By now, my stomach and my brain were both like jelly, and my cough was getting worse. I was miserable.

The replacement belt arrived, and with *a push start* we were off. I didn't offer to help with the pushing.

We got to Bamako at 6.45 p.m. It had been almost *eleven hours*, and I had managed it without eating anything more than Diacalm, or doing anything much else. Now I just had to get to the hotel fast, and as the touts were the least of my problems, I simply pushed through them and got a taxi.

I deserved a break, so - "The Grand Hotel please."

If at all possible, I was going to live in style for a day or two. That was if the Grand Hotel had a room in their new, economical annex, and if they wouldn't mind someone who was looking like death warmed up. And if they would accept payment by Mastercard.

Yes, yes, yes!

The Grand Hotel, Bamako, lived up to its name, and even though the annex was only slightly better than a

Travelodge in Britain, it was grand enough for me. I was even led to it by a porter, who unfortunately expected a tip on the spot, which was difficult since I only had the equivalent of fifteen pence in my pocket. I offered him this, and he looked puzzled, so I promised him that I would have more small change later. He didn't seem to understand the concept of "small change" either.

The room was spotless, with en-suite facilities, and it looked like I was the first customer to be there, which was quite possible as the annex had just opened. All for 25,000 CFAs a night. Ok, that was still way out of my budget, but for a moment I forgot my predicament, threw myself on the bed, and said "YES!"

I had booked for two nights, to start with, and was going to have to get cash soon, but this was going to be good. Even my stomach had settled, or the five Diacalm were at last doing their job. I was left, though with an abiding fear of farting, which was not to leave me.

Since I knew that the hotel had good internet connections, though expensive, I was going to be able, at last, to bring Kate up to date, so once I had made myself look as up-market as possible (freshly washed and ironed tee-shirt - thank you John), I headed to the lobby and booked a terminal. I was very aware that none of the other guests were wearing dirty trainers, or jeans, but nothing was said.

It was oh, so easy to run up a bill for the internet, and just sign for it. What fun! I told Kate the story so far, and promised to email again the next day once I knew what my plan was for getting back to Dakar. I was beginning to flag a bit and was feeling the strain of such a stressful day with no food except the early morning bread, so decided to risk a beer in the bar, though I could still feel rumblings inside.

The bar was posh, though not opulent, and almost deserted. Apart from the barman, chatting to a waitress, there was only one other couple there - a well-dressed, portly, middle aged, white business man, accompanied by a very attractive young African lady in a stunning red dress. I took a bottle of Flag, at twice the price I had ever paid anywhere else, and wedged myself with my thoughts into a corner against the wall. This was just what I wanted, peace and a beer, with a toilet close at hand. I was in defensive mode.

Sipping at the bottle, and mulling over the day, I became aware that though not an argument, the conversation between the business man and his partner was becoming just a little heated, and glanced up in time to see him leave money on the bar, and march out. She looked a little non-plussed, but picked up the money, then turned to me, smiled and came over. Oh God.

"Hello, would you like to buy me a drink?"

This was *NOT* what I wanted. I just wanted a *quiet* beer, and my own musings. My face became as red as it had been after the trip from Timbuktu.

"I'm sorry, but no, I want to be alone." It sounded corny, but worked. As her eyes strayed to my trainers, she wrinkled her pretty nose, wrote me off, turned and wafted out.

As she disappeared through the door, I glanced after her, then back to the barman and raised my eyebrows in a "Did you see that?" kind of way. Within a second, the waitress was over.

"Would you like me to come to your room? What is your number? Will I come?"

"NO, NO, NO. I want to be alone! *Please*."

She took offence, as did the barman on her behalf, and I could tell that it was going to be difficult to get another beer from them that night. I headed for bed, and locked the door.

Lying between those lovely crisp white sheets in that lovely crisp white room, I started to realise that I was worn out. Ok, I had been to Timbuktu, had done it, but there had been a price. The thought of attempting to return to Dakar the way I had come, by train, Alham, and bush taxi, made me feel ill. The thought of taking the *express train* from Bamako to Dakar - a 35 to 40 hour journey on a train "full of thieves" (as I had been told), with no Michael to guide me, *and* with a crummy tummy, made me feel even worse.

I relaxed. To hell with the cost, I would *fly* from Bamako to Dakar. Not only would that give me an extra day or two in Bamako (I was quite sure that I would never in my lifetime return), but would also give me some free time in Dakar before I headed home. It was such a relief to have made that decision.

It was Friday. The next day, I would book a flight for the Monday. That would allow me two days' rest in Bamako, and three days to explore the bits of Dakar I hadn't had time to see before.

I closed my eyes, and sighed. All would be well.

11. PANIC IN BAMAKO

As I woke gently, slowly, between those glorious clean sheets, I could tell there was something wrong. Not physical, but mental. I was feeling "down".

I could certainly say that there was no obvious reason for this. I was in a wonderful modern hotel room, was in no rush to get up, and a hearty breakfast beckoned. Also, I could mentally map out my way home, and it would be fun, wouldn't it? But I was down.

This feeling had sat on my shoulders many times. Always, two days after coming down from a mountain. Mountains make me high, but the aftermath is often a tremendous low. I was low.

Breakfast was not as hearty as I had expected. *Continental* was the name, but it must have been from a pretty small continent. This was no "All you can eat" deal, more "The least we can get away with", and it didn't lighten my mood much, just my wallet by 4,000 CFAs. But my main concern for the day was not breakfast, it was to get tickets back to Dakar, and I had no idea how to get them, so after a short email to Kate, I asked the smart uniformed receptionist if she could help.

"Certainly, sir. When do you want to fly?"

It was such a pleasure to be able to do things in plain English, after days of struggling with French and Pidgin, and my mood started to lift.

"Monday morning please."

She phoned Air Senegal.

"I'm sorry sir, there's nothing tomorrow, or Monday. There might be a seat on a flight at 10.00 p.m. on Tuesday, but you will have to phone them on Tuesday morning to check."

As my mind raced with the ramifications of what she had just told me, my mood again went into a nose-dive. If I left it till Tuesday morning to find out if I could fly that night, and I couldn't, it would mean I would only have two and a bit days to travel overland, which was impossible. The alternative would be to take the train *now* to Dakar, if it hadn't already left, and if it was going at all. Oh, Lord, the way I felt, *that* was impossible too. Or I could rest for two days then hope to travel overland back by my original route, starting on Monday. Oh God, I didn't want to do that either!

I felt sick, and my mind started to go into some kind of state that I had never experienced before. It felt a bit like I was watching myself coming to bits.

"Please, please, is there any other way? Is there another plane?"

My voice sounded a bit far away, and muffled.

"Yes sir, Air Mauritanie fly once a week to Dakar, on a Saturday, but I cannot get them on the phone. You would be better to go to their office and buy a ticket there."

Saturday. It *was* Saturday.

"What time do they fly?"

"I think it's in the evening. You should have time."

Buzz, buzz, buzz. My head was making funny noises as I searched my guide book for the Bamako map. Air Mauritanie's office was way down by the river. I was out the hotel, and waving down a taxi before I knew it. I had to get there in time. They had to have a seat. The flight had to be going. *Buzz buzz.*

The taxi took me to a corner near the airline office. I paid him, jumped out, and sprinted to the building, and stopped. It was closed, and a sign told me that Air Mauritanie had moved!

There was an address, but it meant nothing to me, and didn't feature on my map.

Buzz, buzz. I was starting to crack.

"Taxi!"

Luckily the driver knew where to take me, and I tipped him handsomely in abject gratitude. I *had* to get that flight.

The airline office was cool, blue, and calm. The buzzing grew quieter.

"Can I have a ticket to Dakar this evening, please?"

"Certainly, sir. The flight is at 6.30 p.m. and the cost is 89,000 CFAs."

"Great, one ticket please," I said calmly, though inwardly a gentle enjoyable fizzing feeling was taking over.

"Yes, sir. Cash only please."

Buzz, buzz!

I didn't have cash, I had my card. It had *lots* of money in it. Oh God, what now?

"Please keep that seat for me. I'll be back with cash."

"Yes sir, but please don't be too long, we shut at lunch time for the day."

On the street, I looked up and down. No bank. No ATM. This was the "business area". Surely there must be an ATM near here. *Surely.* I ran. Nothing. By now, I was well aware that I was having some kind of breakdown, but I knew I had to just keep going. *Buzz.*

On a corner was a bank, with an ATM.

Please God, let it work. My pin. My pin. At last I remembered it, and had 100,000 CFAs in my pocket. I walked, not slowly, but slow enough to force my mind and body to relax, and for all the noises to leave my head, and then bought my ticket back to Dakar. Out in the street, tears welled up in my eyes. Another taxi, (I was beginning to feel like a tycoon) and I was back at the hotel. I needed to phone Kate.

A quick text on the internet to ask her to phone at 2.00 p.m. then I cleared my room and sat at reception waiting her call. There was still a background buzz in my head, but I was slowly settling. Spot on two, the phone rang, and I was directed into a cubicle to take my call. Immediately I heard Kate's voice, so far away, I welled up and blubbed. Thank God I was in a cubicle, and not standing at the reception desk. Kate immediately picked up on it, and was soothing. As I recounted all that had happened, she could hear the strain in my voice and became more and more concerned.

"Joe, I'm going to get a ticket and come out to you there."

That sobered me up. My wife was saying that she would drop everything and spend hundreds of pounds to fly out to Bamako, without a visa, to be with me just because I had a cold and a bad stomach - and couldn't handle the pressure.

"No, no. I'm fine, honest. Just tired, I'll be all right once I get to Dakar. It'll be a real holiday there. I'll soon cheer up. I love you. Thank you. I love you."

I then made a wee joke about offering the porter *small change*, and we laughed. I was sad, but relieved to end the call.

I had already paid for two nights, at great expense, so was pleased to find that they were prepared to give me a rebate on the, now to be unused, night. Not only that, they changed the last of my travellers' cheques, and some sterling, so I was sorted, and flush. I left a much larger tip than my finances warranted, and wandered out into the street for a last look at Bamako. Walking down through the heat, the noise, the trash and the people to the "Patisserie Les Delices", a little of the spring came back into my step. Kate had recharged my batteries. Even my cold was starting to lift, though my stomach was still causing me fear.

My last Malian omelette and chips was delicious, and the cool of the patisserie seduced me to simply sit and let Bamako flow past my window, rather than go out looking for it. Also, there was a good toilet in the place.

All too soon it was time to head for the airport. This was a stress since I imagined it would be awash with touts like the bus station, but arriving in yet another taxi, I found that although there was a crowd milling around outside the terminal, there was no hassle.

Since I was quite early (ok, I was anxious), and my stomach was burbling, I sought out the toilets. They were horrendous! They were unusable! They were outside the terminal. Oh, dear. Perhaps there would be better ones inside the departure area. I pushed my way through the crowd, to the terminal door, and was stopped by a security guard. I explained that I had a plane to catch, and was heading for Dakar.

"Flight not on."

"*What?*"

"You not come in. Flight not on."

It was all I could do not to wail. What was I going to do?

"What do you mean? Is it cancelled? Is there another one? How do I get to Dakar?"

"Flight not on - yet."

The penny dropped. I blushed. In Bamako, the airport terminal is small, very small. They don't let you in until the last minute, and then it's a quick scramble to check in and get on the plane. My plane wasn't ready yet. In fact it hadn't actually arrived, so the flight was not yet *on* the board. Ten minutes later, my flight *was* on and I was in, and heading for the toilets, which thankfully were twenty stages up from those outside.

Sitting on the plane, eating a pretty acceptable airline meal was such a novelty, I had to smile. I pictured my first sight of the plane, with its logo of a *paper dart* on the tail, and imagined a giant hand ...

I would have flown on a balloon if that had been all that was available. This was luxury.

The thin, smart business man in the seat beside me seemed reluctant to talk, possibly since I now had straggly *long* hair, and had only half shaved with my little broken razor-head. I had been wearing the same clothes for about three weeks, and it was beginning to show. I had had a shower that day though. I rested my head back on the soft head-rest, closed my eyes, and re-ran my trip so far. Ok, I had made my goal, and got to Timbuktu, but going by that day's events, I guessed that my journey was far from over. I still had a few days in Dakar, and didn't even know where I would be resting my head that night.

It was 9.00 p.m. when we touched down, and dark. I hated arriving in the dark. Everywhere seems so much more menacing, and I remembered my first night in Dakar. Ok, I was street-wise now, but still, you shouldn't arrive in the dark.

The terminal was as chaotic as I remembered, but ignoring the crowd of bogus "official" transport guys, I got a taxi quickly enough at the rank, and then the rip-off began.

6,500 CFAs to the Ganale hotel. The price was extortionate, and the hotel was full!

Another taxi, to the Farid - full. Then the Oceanic - full.

At last, to La Croix du Sud.

The taxi took another 5,000, and the hotel wanted 55,000! For *one night*!

I took it. This was way, way over my budget, but I wasn't going to join the folks in the doorways, and it was getting late. Luckily they could only take me for one night, so I wouldn't be tempted to spend the kids' inheritance over the next few days. It was a pretty good hotel though, and after a very welcome couple of bottles of Flag in its lively young bar, which brought me back to cosmopolitan life, I crawled up to my room and crashed out. I would sort things out in the morning.

12. UNWINDING IN AFRICA

When a hostage is released from captivity, or someone survives a traumatic event, they are often allowed to spend a few days in a *winding down* place, where they can adjust back to normal life. I felt that I needed a bit of that. Oh, I hadn't been a captive, far from it, and by most people's standards, hadn't had a particularly traumatic experience, but by *my* standards, thousands of miles travelled by land, water, sand and air, with a semi-arrest, a raging cold and a treacherous stomach, amounted to a good excuse for a few days R & R.

I was going to enjoy Dakar.

I started with a long lie. No call to prayer here, and I had forgotten to set an alarm, so luxuriated till 9 o'clock in the morning. Ok, so many people wouldn't think that was much of a lie in, but I had been used to 6.30 a.m. starts, or an invitation to religion at 3.00a.m. This was beyond luxury. After a soft warm shower, and a slightly difficult shave (I was still persevering with the broken razor-head), I decided to phone round the hotels in my guide, and get something nice for that night. I deserved it.

I couldn't phone out. I had made the mistake of settling my bill the night before, so… they had disconnected the phone. I should have realised that no matter what, that all-powerful force that oversees our lives had not yet decided to just let me be (or Timbuktu Jimmy had influence even here).

Out in the sweltering heat, I trudged round to the Farid. It was still full. Perhaps it wasn't. Perhaps they just thought I looked too much of a risk for their swanky place. I was a bit less *groomed* than I had been on my first visit to Dakar, and maybe a bit smelly. Perhaps they thought I was a mercenary on the run. I'm sure there were a few around, especially considering what was happening in Cote D'Ivoire. But hey, I was only a wee ancient Scotsman looking for a place to lay my weary head. That cut no ice. (At that moment, ice would have been wonderful).

Walking round every hotel in the book would have killed me, so I started phoning from a booth.

"Sorry, we're full."
"Sorry, we're full."
"Sorry ......"

Surely they couldn't *see* me. It wasn't a video phone - *surely*.

At last, my final try. I had left the Continental to the end, as its review was perhaps a little less enthusiastic than the others.

"Certainly, sir. I look forward to meeting you."

The Continental was not at the top end of the hotel pecking order, but it had a room, and was only a few streets away from Independence Square. I was sure that after all my travels, and all the places I had slept in, this one would hold few surprises. When I got back to the Croix du Sud for my gear, I found that they had already cleaned and tidied my room. My pack was at reception and I felt that I was being *put out the house.* They seemed to be erasing all trace. This did little for my ego. Hopefully, the Continental would be a bit more welcoming.

It was, and the manager/receptionist/cleaner was chatty as he showed me to my room. It was basic, and not en-suite, but any port in a storm... In fact it had the air of being like a "Fishermen's Mission", rather than a tourist hotel. I certainly didn't expect to bump into many rich Americans. Since this was not a place to spend a lot of leisure time - there was no pool, terrace, lounge or cool veranda - I decided to have a snack at my wee favourite café in the square then head out West to see what Yoff was like.

I had read that Yoff was a very colourful and interesting fishing village on the west of Dakar. It was in fact pretty well a suburb of the city, and was only a short taxi drive away.

The beach is the furthest west you can go on the coast of Africa. It's wide and sandy and there is little to stop a wave from America before it crashes onto the shore. This is not a desolate, windswept lonely place. Far from it. It teems with life. Hundreds of long banana-shaped fishing boats are hauled up on the sand, some being repaired, some resting, and some waiting to be launched into the swell. Almost all of them have a strip of brightly painted designs along each side, just below the gunwale, which is probably specific to each owner. Among them, fishermen, fish buyers, fish sellers, donkeys, carts, footballers and kids throng, work, talk and play. There were no ice cream vans, no "kiss me quick" hats, and only one tourist, me.

I walked about a mile along the beach, through this almost overwhelming sight, and no one tried to sell me anything, not even fish. There were no touts, no hassle merchants, no threats, just smiles, and the occasional "Ca vas?" Most people seemed quite shy of me, a stranger, but when I asked "Malik" if he would take a photo of me on my camera, I was surprised that he was prepared to chat, in reasonable English. He simply talked. He had nothing he wished from me. He didn't want money, and he didn't want to emigrate to Britain. It was refreshing not to feel hustled.

I enjoyed the beach so much that I decided to spend the following day and night in Yoff, so rang the bell at the corrugated iron gate of the *Campement*, which backed on to the beach, and verbally booked a room for the following night without looking inside. My guide book suggested that it was a good place to stay. Since I had already stayed in a place called "Campement" in Mopti, I should have been forewarned.

That done, and feeling relaxed, I wandered through a few of the neighbouring streets, and came upon a wonderful little modern hotel with a proper foyer, a bar, pool and magnificent views of the Atlantic rollers breaking on the rocks below. It seemed a perfect setting and I regretted having committed myself to the Campement. I asked the price and at 20,000 CFAs a night, with breakfast, it seemed too good to be true. I did wonder why it was so empty, and how they came to have so much spare room. I had even been offered a choice.

Then I heard the noise. It was like a distant roll of thunder, but it didn't stop. It grew and grew until it filled the hotel, and I ducked. A giant passenger jet skimmed the roof top. We weren't just on the flight path for Dakar Airport, we were almost part of the runway! I must have arrived in Yoff during a lull in flights, or just hadn't noticed them up till then. I noticed them now. The receptionist was unmoved.

Ok, I was committed to the Campement in Yoff for the next night, and would sort out the remaining nights later. Meanwhile, back to say hello to the vultures again at the top of the Independence, and omelette in the Imperial. I was getting used to this.

You should never let yourself become too complacent or confident.

It was late when I finished people-watching from my perch in the café, and, like the Oceanic, the Continental was a few very dark streets away. Oh, I wasn't scared of the dark now. I had been to Timbuktu, and back. I knew my way around.

"Hello, it's good to see you. I'm the receptionist in your hotel. I recognise you. Do you recognise me?"

He was six foot three, unshaved, and wearing a hoodie - in Dakar!

"No, sorry, I don't recognise you. I think you've got the wrong person."

"No, no, sir, I am your receptionist. I remember you."

This was a scam which was actually mentioned in the guide book. He would next tell me that he was my friend, take me to a "party", then drug and mug me. The book told me so. He was working to a script.

"Ok, tell me, what hotel am I in?"

"Eh, the Ganale"

"Try again."

"Oh, I meant the Ganale Independence."

"No. Listen, you are *not* the receptionist in my hotel, and ...."

I realised that whether he was *my* receptionist, or *anyone's* receptionist, he was still six foot three, and standing between me and my hotel, three very dark streets away.

"Mister, *I am not lying to you*."

"TAXI!"

Luckily, a taxi pulled up immediately, with a grizzled old man at the wheel. I leaned over to his window and whispered "Continental Hotel please."

"What is a hotel?" he replied in a weird French accent.

"*What?*"

"What is a hotel?"

"God help me." I thought, and decided to return to the lights of the Imperial, have another beer and abandon myself to my fate, and this big lying mugger.

"Mister, get in, get in."

No matter what, the driver was not going to lose me to the competition, so I climbed in.

"You show me hotel."

Ah. This was better. I directed him the few hundred yards to the Continental, and then pointed to the "Hotel" sign.

"That's a hotel."

I actually gave him a tip for saving me from a fate worse than death, but later realised that it had all been a linguistic misunderstanding, and he was saying "What hotel?" not "What is a hotel?" Ho, hum, you learn. Slowly. That night I employed my sleeping bag and mosquito net to their full. It was that kind of place.

The breakfast next morning was meagre coffee and bread, but the company was good. My eating companions were two Ghanaian sailors, and a Senegalese businessman. All three were young, well-travelled, and articulate in English. One of the Ghanaians was a navigator and had particularly good English. The Senegalese was an importer of fruit juice, which amazed me, as I had imagined that Senegal would have been able to produce all the fruit juice it needed. As I bemoaned the constant hassle and hustle I had experienced on my trip, the navigator assured me that it wasn't just because I was white, or a tourist. He explained that he too had the same trouble because he spoke English, Ghana being an Anglophone country.

Unfortunately this little unusual interlude of simple chat had to end all too soon for me, as my companions were working men and had to get on. I, on the other hand, had a day to kill before I sampled the delights of the Campement, Yoff, so I wandered central Dakar, soaking in the sights and sounds, aware that my days in Africa were numbered, and that I might never return.

Again I watched the doll sellers in Independence Square, and promised myself that one of them would be going home with me (a doll, not the seller). There was a light interlude while I watched a poor, pale-faced little tourist man, being chased from one bench to another by a shoe-shine boy. The tourist had obviously been told by his wife to wait for her in the square, so couldn't escape, and the little boy wouldn't take "no" for an answer. The boy won. He never bothered me though. I was wearing very dirty trainers. I emailed Kate, and downloaded to her my escapades so far. I also assured her that the buzzing in my head had stopped, and that I was as sane as usual again. I was looking forward to seeing her.

There were four more nights before I would be flying home; that night in Yoff, two on Goree, I had decided, and my final night would be in Dakar.

Yoff was booked. I phoned the Hostellerie du Chevalier de Bouffliers on Goree.

"Certainly, sir. Two nights. You will be in room five.

Sorted.

Next, for my final African night. I phoned round. As usual, full, full, full.

Eventually, I was able to book a night in the Miramar, a medium price, central city hotel. Phew. All I had to do now was enjoy myself.

Yet another taxi took me out to Yoff, and I had my first sight of my room in the Campement. The first thing that I noticed was the noise of flies, hundreds of them, both in my room, and all throughout the place, which was built like a square, single storey compound, with a dry ornamental pond in the middle. Mac's it wasn't. Perhaps, at least, the noise of the flies would mask the sound of the aircraft. The second thing I noticed was the smell. Now, I had expected a bit of a whiff of fish, since Yoff is very much a fishing village, and I had smelled North Eastern Scottish fishing villages in the past, but this was different. If this was the smell of the fish, I would be sticking to omelettes.

I was booked. I was here, and at least I could look forward to the *next* two nights on Goree, which promised much, so I decided to put up with a little discomfort to allow me to enjoy a few hours in the vibrancy of Yoff beach. Anyway, it was only 7,000 CFAs for the night, including breakfast. Can't say fairer than that.

As quickly as possible, I sorted out my bed with sleeping bag (*there was no way I was going to touch the sheets)*, and mosquito net (*hopefully strong enough to keep the flies out)*, and climbed up a few steps to the dining area which was a scrappy, dark wooden hut-like structure with windows overlooking the beach. Now I learned what the smell was. It was nothing to do with the fish. Outside the window was a corrugated iron roof which covered a shed on the beach down below. It was baking hot, and this was where several cats lived, *and toileted*. I had certainly heard of "Cat on a hot tin roof", but this was *cats'* on a hot tin roof, and it stank! The window was open. I bought a Fanta, at an inflated price, and almost ran out of the place.

The beach, even if it was strewn with many dead fish, was like a breath of fresh air. As usual, there were football matches in all directions, in fact they appeared to stretch almost unbroken along the beach, off into the haze two or three miles to the north.

The one being played on a semi-official pitch, just at the entrance to the beach, was a serious affair, with a real football and one of the teams actually wearing football strips.

Apart from the goalie, they all appeared to be number 11, and called Ronaldo.

It was an exciting match and I was left in peace to watch for a while.

The fish-market area itself was alive with activity, and I was allowed to take photos of the women sitting by their stalls which consisted of long lines of polystyrene fish-boxes, crammed with everything from sprats to huge swordfish which were a sad sight.

People seemed interested in me from a distance, but only smiled in my direction, without approaching, which was refreshing. There was one point, however, when I would have liked to ask for an explanation, but was too shy - one of the many horse and carts came past me, and attached to the single axle on the cart, just behind the horse, was a *fan*! I couldn't tell whether this was a visual joke, or fulfilled some practical purpose.

I pondered if there was a French equivalent of "When the ... hits the fan". At least it gave me a smile to take to bed.

Sitting with my back to a huge painted banana-boat, drinking my Fanta and watching the sun set over the Atlantic, with the breaking swell crashing on the beach feet away, was amazing. I would have thrown my clothes off and rushed in if there hadn't been three hundred other people there, most of whom had probably used the beach as a toilet within the last twenty four hours. It wasn't a *swimming* beach. Eventually, of course, it was dark, and I had to leave and head to the *pit*. At least the flies seemed to be in bed (theirs) before me, and the smell had subsided with the temperature.

The flies were early risers, unlike the management, and in the morning, after an urgent dash across the dusty yard to the toilet opposite (my stomach was still my worst enemy), I sat for half an hour watching the cats from the restaurant window. Amazingly, my hunger survived the spectacle, and when Malik arrived, I was ready for breakfast. I must have been ravenous, since even he didn't put me off. In other circumstances, unshaven, in last night's clothes, and a bit food splattered, he would have been a real deterrent, but I *was hungry*.

Even so, I only managed coffee and lots of bread and jam. I decided not to try the ham, which may well have been ok, but then again.... My stomach was bad enough. My main thought was to leave as soon as possible, but first I had to have a rather loud argument with Malik who decided to charge me an extra 1,000 CFAs for the breakfast. I won. I wouldn't be back.

Since I was now heading for Goree, to what looked like a really nice, up-market bijou-style hotel, I put on my best white tee-shirt. It was "best" because it was clean. I wanted to make an impression (hopefully the lingering cat smell would have dissipated by the time I got there).

It was easy to wave down a taxi on the main road, and I was soon speeding back towards central Dakar. Speeding was exactly it. Speeding, with no hands on the wheel. The driver liked to tell a good story, even if it was in French and it was obvious that I didn't understand a word and, of course, all good French stories are accompanied by much arm waving and gesticulations. Perhaps he was the same driver who had picked me up all that time ago from the airport when I first arrived in Africa. Perhaps they all drove like that. Within a minute I had located the seat belt, and much to the driver's amusement, strapped myself in as tightly as I could.

I realised my mistake as I stepped out, white faced in Independence Square.

Slashing diagonally across my erstwhile pristine tee-shirt was a beautifully sharp and clear black sash of dirt! It was likely that the only use that the seat belt had ever seen, up till the point that I put it on, was as a dirt-magnet. To add insult to injury, the driver gave me his card because he was "*best driver*", and I might want him again. I then looked further down, and discovered that the zip on my fly had burst open, and looked irreparable. After weeks of sweaty travelling in the same clothes they were starting to disintegrate. I was now a mess. I had forgotten to shave. Luckily there were no muddy puddles for me to trip and fall into.

I turned my tee-shirt inside out, and pulled it down as far as it would go to cover my errant zip. That was as respectable as I was going to get for a while.

Much as I was eager to get to Goree, and peace, I had some shopping to do in the city first, so I left my bag at the reception desk of the Independence, and headed out. Internet first, and caught up with Kate's news. I kept sending her love and kisses, and realised that I was feeling *happy*. Next, I bought a whole bottle of wine (what luxury), a corkscrew (I had no idea what the carry-out arrangements would be on Goree), and at last, a decent razor.

That was me sorted for a couple of days' R & R on a paradise island.

Back at the Independence, over a morning beer on the roof, I decided that I really would have to spruce myself up a bit, so off came the tee-shirt, and was given a good swish in the swimming pool. I didn't use soap, since that might have shown up on the surface, and anyway, I didn't have any. Next off came the trousers, and sitting in my rather worn underpants, I took out my emergency tool kit, and sewed the zip back on the fly. Luckily, since I was sitting next to a swimming pool, the sight of me in only my pants didn't seem to register with the few tourists who appeared. My tee-shirt soon dried in the breeze, and to my eye, was fit for purpose. Once sorted, I had what was maybe going to be my last look down at the square from the top of the Independence. Still the hawks flew round the Indy tower, while the hawkers stalked below. I would remember that scene.

A leisurely lunch in the square and then a very busy ferry trip, saw me on Goree, mid-afternoon. It was all as I had remembered it - a haven, albeit a tourist-filled haven.

Needless to say, when I presented myself at the reception of the wonderful Hostellerie du Chevalier de Bouffliers, the receptionist took one look at me, and couldn't find my name on the register. However I was *not* going to be put off. I had travelled far, and dreamt about this place for days. I was going to stay here. I had booked by phone. They had said "Yes, we will give you room 5." It would be mine. I told him all this.

He gave me room 5.

It was wonderful.

On the first floor of a separate annex in an old colonial style building in a bougainvillea-draped alleyway at the back of the hotel, the room itself was huge, with two double beds, three soft seats, one lounger/couch, one big wooden desk, one large wardrobe, and space to dance. The whole theme was beige walls and blue/white coverings and carpets on a painted wooden floor. There was a ceiling fan and pristine white mosquito nets over each bed. There was also a *real* candle on the bedside table.

This was like a honeymoon suite (though a honeymoon suite with two double beds - mmm), and I wished Kate could just *be* there. The only downside was that the toilet facilities were separated from the bed area by a half-height wall. An informal set-up. The first thing I did was shave. With my new *sharp* razor, complete with handle, I performed this oh-so-necessary task with no fear of dropping the scraper down the plug-hole. Life could not get better. I then showered, lit the candle and lay on one of the beds, drinking red wine, feeling a lovely gentle breeze from the window, and thinking of Kate. This was where I wanted her to be.

I promised myself that one day I would bring her there.

From my first day on Goree, which seemed to be years before, I had looked forward to being on the island, and as I later wandered to the castle I felt more at peace and easy within myself than I had for a long time. The castle was actually an old fortified gun emplacement from World War II times, and the underground bunkers housed a whole community of people. They were mostly artists and crafts people, and served a busy tourist trade each day. In the evening, they came out of their holes and the whole area had a laid-back hippy feel to it, but was clean, and even sported some small green gardens where the guns used to be. The art, mostly small works of oil on canvas, depicting stylised African people, appeared to be all from the same school. They had obviously found what was popular with the tourists. I bought a couple, and then watched the sunset over the Dakar skyline off to the west, to the sound of not so distant drumming. There was a drumming school further down the hill.

I was in no rush to explore further, since there would be plenty time to do so the next day, and ambled back towards the hotel, stopping for a supper of grilled fish and chips, washed down with beer, in a restaurant by the beach. I made sure to go nowhere near Mama Kine's place though. Necklaces and hassle I did not want.

As the tourists left, it felt as if a gate had been closed, and Goree became a village in its own right, of which I was privileged to be a small, if temporary, part.

Later, sitting at a little table on the hotel terrace, in the dark, overlooking a sea-swished beach, I sipped a cool wine, and waited for a phone call from Kate. I had told the receptionist that my wife might phone me about nine o'clock, but he looked rather blank, as if he didn't understand. At nine, the phone rang, he answered it, scowled, and handed it to me.

Talking to Kate was wonderful. I had so much to tell, and to ask, but after five minutes, the receptionist returned with a colleague and they both started giving me unfriendly looks. It was then that I realised that I was hogging the only phone in the hotel, and blocking their line. Sadly, I wished Kate goodnight.

The next hour was spent simply *chilling* on the terrace. This was a world away from how I had been living for the last three weeks, and I was going to enjoy every moment of it.

I woke the next day, wondering where I was. Had I died? Was this heaven? I lay, remembering my first morning in Dakar, lying looking at the spiders' webs, and listening to goats bleating. Now it was clean white ceiling and the gentle sound of distant waves. Perhaps it *was* heaven.

My day consisted of lazily wandering around the island, chatting with the artists, visiting the little museum (there was a strong history of slavery), and talking, over lunch to a couple of young American missionaries. They had been evacuated from Cote D'Ivoire a week before, and now were holed up in a guest house in Dakar. The girl's mum and dad had flown from America to join them to check that they were ok. Some of these missionaries take big risks.

After lunch, I discovered "The Goree Institute". This was a large, but simple, two-storey building, hidden away behind palm trees near my hotel. I was intrigued, and assumed it was like a community centre, so wandered in. I didn't get far. A rather large, strong, and to me, menacing guy appeared and simply informed me that I should leave, *NOW*.

I left.

In retrospect, I decided that it had been a Madrassa or some such thing, where white Westerners might look a bit out of place. It didn't matter. The rest of the island was a little paradise.

I treated myself to the best meal I had had for weeks (steak, chips, ice cream, and half a bottle of wine, on the terrace). Idyllic, and I ended the day as I had the previous one, simply sitting, being. It would be my last night on Goree, possibly forever. I almost wept.

In the morning I had to leave, and I knew I had run up quite a bill, but what the hell, it was worth it. I could pay off my card later when all was over. I lingered as long as possible over my packing, but eventually made my way to reception to settle up.

"TRANSACTION REFUSED".

That's what it said. *My credit card was not working anymore!*

I asked the receptionist to try it again. He did. It didn't work.

It would have been folly to carry on. Three strikes and you're out, they say, and the nearest branch of HSBC, as far as I knew, was in Aberdeen! Once I had counted out the cash from my wallet, I was left with enough to pay for the ferry, and very little else. I had no other resources. If my card was dead, so was I.

I still had one more night to pass in Dakar, not to mention I had to eat, and somehow get to the airport the next day. The 500 CFAs left in my wallet weren't going to cover that.

The plan had been that I would spend half the day on Goree, and then make my way to the Miramar Hotel which was booked for my last night in Dakar, but now I *had* to get to Dakar as soon as I could to try to reinvigorate my card. If I couldn't, I would be sleeping rough, and hungry in the street with the other people of the night (did I fancy that?), and then it would be a long walk to the airport. I really didn't want my big adventure to end that way (though I did recognise that it might be quite exciting - *what was I thinking*?)

The ferry trip back over, which should have been enjoyable, was anything but. I felt sick, not from the sea, but from the thought that my rotten HSBC card was again a traitor. The temptation was to chuck the thing overboard as I had done with my errant torch/alarm. Luckily, I didn't.

Stressed as I was, I decided to check in to the Miramar before I attempted to fix my finances.

"I'm sorry sir, we have no note of your booking, and we're full up."

I was getting used to the script. Ok, I was a bit scruffy, a bit ragged round the edges, but I *had* booked, and they knew it. I protested. I pleaded. I panicked. The Miramar, being a big, poshish city hotel, had staff who didn't give in easily.

"Sorry sir, we have no rooms left."

So now it was - no money *and* no hotel. The holiday was not ending well.

"*Please.*"

"I'll try and find you some place sir."

Eventually, he got me a place in the Ganale, and suggested I should go there right away to book in. I thanked him, and gave him my 500 CFAs. I was now destitute.

The Ganale was a nice enough hotel, which could have been anywhere, and was going to be my last resting place in Africa. At least I had a bed.

Now, urgently, I had to get cash. It would be too dangerous to try an ATM in case the card got swallowed, so I put my trust in a bank teller.

"Yes sir, how much do you want?"

I chanced it "A hundred thousand CFAs please."

"Certainly sir, please enter your number in the machine," and he counted out the cash.

I was rich again.

While I enjoyed a celebratory beer in the Imperial, a hawker came in and tried to sell me several small birds. I didn't know if they were intended as pets, or were for eating, but since I had just had an omelette, I declined. He went away looking really crestfallen. *What did he expect?*

13. A SETTING SUN

It slowly began to sink in that my big adventure was drawing to a close. The next day I would be heading home. Excitement, anticipation, and sadness. I emailed Kate, to say how much I was looking forward to holding her again, then wandered pretty aimlessly, trying hard to take in as much as possible of the strange atmosphere of Dakar. Tomorrow, I would be in rainy, cold Scotland. Home.

I could well remember the same feeling from the last days of holidays in my childhood.

Although my flight wasn't till late in the afternoon the next day, I went to bed early, and lay awake for a long time, playing my mind-video, and running some scenes over and over again. Had I really *done that*? Had I really been to *Timbuktu*?

And then it was my last day, and I was going to soak in as much sun as possible to take back with me. But first, a task. I had a doll to buy.

I knew exactly how to go about this. Just sit in the middle of Independence Square in Dakar, and a doll seller will be by your side in a minute. She was probably only about thirteen, but was pretty, and dressed in swathes of red and gold cloth. On her head was what appeared to be a little turban of the same material, which was topped off with a straw basket full of dolls, all miniature copies of her herself. She seemed surprised that I didn't shoo her away, but indicated that she should lay her basket on the bench so that I could choose. Her price was 2,000 CFAs per doll, but once I had chosen, I gave her 5,000, and wished her well. Now she was even more surprised. Normally she would have been haggled down to half her price, but I had given her much more. What else could I do? I had a daughter and at the same age, she had made and sold little felt mice for pocket money. This girl was selling for food. She smiled, but said nothing as she walked away, and then I saw her stop, turn, and come back. I thought she would now try to sell me another doll, but I had, not for the first time, misjudged human nature. She smiled again, and handed me an exquisite little beaded necklace, then quickly left.

I had a warm glow as I watched her go.

My last experience of Dakar was not African. It was pure, posh Western. The Teranga Hotel was exclusive, expensive, luxurious, and not really for the likes of me, but I went there, marched in as if I owned the place, and took up residence at a nice table near the pool, with a view over to the ocean. This was where I intended to spend my last hours. I defied anyone to say otherwise. Since being again *in the money,* and able to pay their ridiculous prices for beer and sandwiches, I was tolerated, though told that the pool was for members only. They were in no danger, my bag with my swimming trunks was left at the Independence, and this was not a place where I would have ventured a swim in my pants.

Abba was playing, everyone was white, and Africa was being drained out of me. I tried to let it go. I couldn't take it with me, could I?

Too soon, I was just another tourist on a plane heading back to Aberdeen.

I brought Africa with me.

I couldn't help it, could I?

After a huge long, warm hug with my wife, I kissed my daughter, and she said,

"How was it dad?"

"A dawdle." I replied.

POSTSCRIPT

A couple of years after I had come back from Timbuktu, I read that great things were planned there. A lot of aid money was to be ploughed into the place, and a major seat of Islamic learning was to be created, along with good tourist hotels and facilities. There was even word that the canal, which once linked the town with the Niger River, would be re-dug, and opened for traffic.

I resolved that for my seventieth birthday, I would return to see all these wonders.

Unfortunately, in early 2012, the Tuaregs started a new rebellion, in which they were joined by fighters returning from the Libyan uprising. These fighters brought with them a good supply of weapons, and fairly soon the Malian army was defeated in the North of the country, including the town of Timbuktu.

Soon after this, the Malian government was overthrown in a coup, and at the same time, militant Islamists took control of the rebellion, side-lining the Tuaregs. These Islamists then proclaimed that Timbuktu would be subject to Sharia Law, including the veiling of women, stoning of adulterers, mutilation of thieves, etc.

Anything which was deemed to be against the teaching of Islam was banned, and pictures appeared in the news of a great deal of destruction being wrought in the town.

I wondered what might now be the state of The Sahara Passion and the other hotels, and especially of the Amanar Restaurant and my friend Tamimou. I was sure that Jimmy, Toré and the rest of the Timbuktu "Mafia" would have survived.

Even though the French army has now helped the Malian troops to chase out the "Bad Guys", It doesn't look like I will be able to return any time soon to find out.

ABOUT THE AUTHOR

Joe Lindsay lives in the pretty little village of North Kessock, in the North of Scotland. He has spent most of his working life in civil engineering, but at the age of 50, decided that enough was enough. He became a Targemaker, and spent the next 19 years making more than 2000 exquisite replicas of the old Jacobite Highlanders' shields, which are now throughout the world.

Unfortunately, arthritis has put an end to his craft, but not to his wish to create, so he is now entering into the world of literature.

Although he has written many short children's stories privately for the delight of his grandchildren, this book is his first venture into publishing, and his hope is that it will give as much pleasure to its readers as his targes did to their owners.